Persistent Voices

POETRY BY

WRITERS LOST

TO AIDS

Edited by

Philip Clark and David Groff

ALYSON*books*

Persistent Voices
Poetry by Writers Lost to AIDS

Copyright © 2009 by Philip Clark and David Groff
Preface © 2009 by Kim Addonizio
Introduction © 2009 by Philip Clark and David Groff

Permission acknowledgments and copyright history and for the individual poems can be found on page 276–282.

Published by Alyson Books
245 West 17th Street, Suite 1200, New York, NY 10011

ALYSON*books*

ISBN-10: 1-59350-153-6
ISBN-13: 978-1-59350-153-2

Cover design by Scott Idleman
Book interior by Elyse Strongin, Neuwirth & Associates, Inc.

Printed in the United States of America
Distributed by Consortium Book Sales and Distribution
Distribution in the United Kingdom by Turnaround Publisher

CONTENTS

THE POETS

PREFACE

Kim Addonizio

IN THE EARLY 1990s, another poet, Beret Strong, and I decided
to offer a free workshop for people with HIV/AIDS. We got per-
mission to use a room in San Francisco's Davies Hospital, got
the word out by posting flyers around town, and ended up with
a core group of four to seven men who came regularly to read
their work and to talk about their illness, their lives, and poetry.
It was a small gesture that we made, as teachers and poets, in
response to what was going on all around us. The Castro was full
of gaunt men. They walked slowly with the aid of another man's
arm around their shoulders, or were pushed along in wheel-
chairs, bundled in blankets even on warm days. Everyone seemed
to know someone who had died, or was dying. Getting out of my
car in the hospital parking lot one afternoon, I watched a man
carry another in his arms, up the hill away from the hospital—
was he taking him home to die? Had they been turned away for
lack of insurance? There was no way to know. I went inside and
tried to help the students in our workshop tell their own stories,
because they needed to tell them, because they wanted someone
to know who they were, because they wanted to create something
out of the circumstances of their lives.

A writing group for the dying—and these men were dying; all
but one would be gone within the next couple of years—might

appear to be a grim enterprise. But what I remember from the workshop belies that idea. There was sorrow, of course; one man whose lover also had AIDS described their arguments over which of them would die first. A man in his twenties was reeling from his recent diagnosis. But beyond that, beyond the fear of death and the humiliations of the body, there were jokes and laughter, and a sense of a shared endeavor. There were intense discussions about word choices and metaphors, about line breaks and imagery, interrupted by the occasional Code Blue being called over the intercom. There was something I can only call attention: the moment attended to, experienced, lived in.

So it is with this anthology of poets. Poetry is a record of consciousness, bearing witness to life fully lived, and as such it can transcend even death. Poems bring us the spirits of those who wrote them. Those spirits are variously amused, grieving, angry, longing, observing, questioning. They are here, in these pages, available to us. We encounter them each time we read their words. For anyone with HIV or affected by it, and for those who have not encountered it before, this anthology is a love letter: to you, for you, who are mortal and alive, paying attention to our brief hour.

ACKNOWLEDGMENTS

Our thanks to all those people who made this book possible and ensured that these poets' voices would be heard. Our gratitude first to the book's agents, Frances Goldin and Sam Stoloff, who took on this project out of the goodness of their hearts and found it the right home. Don Weise, the publisher of Alyson Books, edited the book with a keen appreciation for poetry, and published it with panache. His team at Alyson, Paul Florez and designer Scott Idleman of Blink Design, were also essential to getting it done on time and beautifully. We are glad as well for the people who brought the two of us together to work on this project: Robert Cabell, Craig Hickman, and David Rosen. We offer our appreciation to Ron Padgett and Keith McDermott for allowing us to use the poignant art of Joe Brainard on our cover. And our deep thanks to Kim Addonizio for volunteering her affecting foreword.

The executors and rights holders of the poets' estates unhesitatingly gave us permission to reprint these poems. We are grateful to them for foregoing reprint fees and joining with us in a charitable donation: The editors' advance monies (less minor expenses) and all royalties earned on *Persistent Voices* are being donated to the PEN Fund for Writers and Editors with AIDS.

Many people were instrumental in bringing together the poets in this anthology. The executors along with many other people made suggestions on which poets and poems to include, facilitated obtaining permission for these poems, introduced us to poets whose work we did not know but whose poems moved us, and encouraged and supported us along the way. Vital to the shape and success of this book are Alysia Abbott, Dr. Leonard Alberts, Frederick Luis Aldama, Kathleen L. Barber, Greg Baysans, Dodie Bellamy, David Bergman, Jeremy Bigalke, Constant Boesen, Christopher Bram, Michael Bronski, Victor Bumbalo, Jorge Camacho, Janine Canan, Michael Canter, Tom Cardamone, Lázaro Gómez Carriles, Justin Chin, Henri Cole, Michael Connor, Dennis Cooper, Jim Cory, David Cobb Craig, Jameson Currier, jw curry, Gavin Geoffrey Dillard, Deanna Dixon, Mark Doty, Deyanira Escobar, Edward Field, Gregory Ford, Craig Gidney, Jonathan Greene, Rachel Hadas, Gerald Hannon, Sean Harvey, Gwen Head, Trebor Healey, Daniel Healy, Pam Heaton, Greg Herren, Cliff Hickman, Richard Howard, Marie Howe, Robin Howe, Philip Huang, Ed Jackson, Saeed Jones, Keith Kahla, Nicolás Kanellos, Michele Karlsberg, Marita Keilson-Lauritz, Kevin Killian, Susan King, Jan B. Kirk, Adam Klein, Michael Klein, the late Dolores Koch, Gerard Koch, Gloria Koch, Joan Larkin, Winston Leyland, Chip Livingston, Maz Livingston, Timothy Liu, Barry Lloyd, Stefan Lynch, Jaime Manrique, Adrianne Marcus, Jim Marks, Kevin Martin, Donna Masini, Richard McCann, J.D. McClatchy, Patrick Merla, Diane Middlebrook, E. Ethelbert Miller, Greg Miller, Jim Mitchell, William Mohr, Sean Monohan, Honor Moore, Lisa C. Moore, James Nolan, Ron Padgett, Nancy Peters, Robert Philen, Dennis Phillips, Barbara L. Pieniadz, Kirk Read, Richard Reitsma, Michael Roberts, Harold McNeil Robinson, Jerry Rosco, Margaret Sand, Michael Schmidt, Bob Sharrard, the late Reginald Shepherd, Susan Sherman, Charley Shively, Aaron Shurin, Ron Silliman, Ira Silverberg, Dr. Charles Silverstein, Mary Alice Sims, Aaron Smith, Mark Tambella, Susan Tracz, David Trinidad, Richard Turley, Peter van Haassen, Jan VanStavern, Wendy Weil,

Bernard Welt, the late Jonathan Williams, Christopher Wiss, Terry Wolverton, Gregory Woods, Warren Keith Wright, Ian Young, and Sean Yule.

Philip would like to thank his parents for their patience as he buried himself in this project for over four years. His sincere thanks go to all of those friends who asked smart questions and listened as he discussed, at great length, the highs and lows of putting *Persistent Voices* together. Finally, Philip first read many of these poets in high school, when he found their books on the library shelves at a gay youth group in Washington D.C.; he would like to thank all those who work for and mentor gay youth, helping guide them toward, in the words of E.M. Forster, "a happier year."

David thanks his partner, Clay Williams, and the poets in this book he knew and whose support and example sustain him: Tory Dent, Melvin Dixon, Tim Dlugos, Paul Monette, and Reginald Shepherd.

We are grateful to every poet in this anthology. Their words persist for all of us.

INTRODUCTION

Philip Clark and David Groff

WE HAVE LOST some of our best poets to AIDS—but they have left us a legacy of affecting and enduring poems. From Steve Abbott to Tory Dent and James Merrill to Donald Woods, *Persistent Voices* celebrates their lives and presents their poems—often dealing with AIDS, but also with other vital subjects—in the context of an unremitting epidemic that is claiming millions of lives and devastating world culture. Let *Persistent Voices* provide an introduction and testament to voices whose urgent eloquence calls to us today.

As editors of this anthology, we approach these poets and their work from different times and different perspectives. David, a poet and editor who came of age amid AIDS, knew and worked with a number of these writers; he was present as AIDS wreaked its havoc in America's and the world's artistic communities. Philip, a writer and researcher born less than a year before the first AIDS cases were publicized, discovered many of these poets in high school, taking sustenance from their works while growing up as a young gay man. What we share is a deep appreciation for these writers' words and visions and a passion that their lives and work never be forgotten.

The forty-five poets in *Persistent Voices* offer us only a small number of the fine writers who have died of AIDS. There are many more poets whose work we considered and did not have space to include, and we hope readers will seek out their work, as well as other writing by the poets we were able to publish. The poets in this anthology range from such well-known and highly regarded figures as Reinaldo Arenas, Tory Dent, Essex Hemphill, James Merrill, Paul Monette, and Reginald Shepherd to those less well-known but long prized by readers and poets: Thomas Avena, Donald Britton, David Matias, Jack Sharpless, and others. It also brings to the attention of readers the work of poets who were largely unknown in their lifetimes, many of whom died of AIDS before they could fulfill their promise. These poets include Sam D'Allesandro, who has since achieved renown with the short stories from his book *The Zombie Pit*; David Craig Austin, a Columbia University student whose only collection, still unpublished, is housed in that school's archives; Chasen Gaver, whose wild Washington D.C. performances pre-dated the popularity of slam poetry; and England's Adam Johnson, who published a chapbook and three full-length collections before dying at the age of twenty-eight. Several of these writers are known more for their prose than their poetry, among them Reinaldo Arenas, the Cuban novelist and memoirist who wrote *Before Night Falls*; Cookie Mueller, who was one of the apostles of the East Village arts movements in the 1970s and 1980s; and George Whitmore, author of the novel *Nebraska* as well as the pioneering work of journalism, *Someone Was Here: Profiles in the AIDS Epidemic*. Including their poetry in this anthology allows us to see all their work in a new way.

Two of these forty-five writers are women: Cookie Mueller and Tory Dent, who in her books *HIV, Mon Amour*, and *Black Milk* was one of the fiercest and most intense chroniclers of AIDS in poetry. Millions of women around the planet have confronted AIDS and HIV, often in dire or hopeless circumstances, and we honor their lives and their contributions. Whatever the sex or sexuality of the writers in *Persistent Voices*—and most of the men in this anthology identified themselves as gay—they exhibit vast geographic and aesthetic breadth. *Persistent Voices* includes such international writers as Arenas, Johnson, the Canadians Don Garner and Michael Lynch, and Jaime Gil de Biedma, a Spanish poet. American poets concerned with urban spaces, such as Walta Borawski and Daniel Diamond, sit beside those who often spoke of rural or small-town lives, like Steve Abbott and Leland Hickman. Styles represented in *Persistent Voices* range from the measured yet piercingly personal poetry of Melvin Dixon, William Dickey, and James Merrill to the more pop-culture, organic-form, and often sexually explicit poets of the West Coast and New York's East Village, such as Joe Brainard, the esteemed Pop Art illustrator and collage artist, and Gil Cuadros, a Chicano chronicler of life in 1980s and early 1990s Los Angeles. Many Hispanic-American, African-American, and Caribbean-American poets are also included, Arturo Islas, Roy Gonsalves, and Assotto Saint among them.

Persistent Voices is not an anthology of poems about AIDS, although many of the poets included here do confront AIDS, directly or obliquely. For some of these writers, HIV was a central factor in their lives and work; others dealt with it implicitly or not at all, and still others, ambushed by the disease, did not live long enough to write about it. Those poets who took HIV as their topic write with often breathtaking power and force, employing extremely different approaches toward the intense and intensely personal experience of AIDS. The AIDS poems in this volume range from Dent's knotted, cascading, and often brutal inclusiveness to Melvin Dixon's keen, precise tolling of the clock and the keening elegies and forthrightly political poems of Paul Monette, whose *Love Alone* both memorialized his late partner and attacked the society that allowed him to die. But in fact, a majority of the poems included here are not about AIDS at all; their concerns, like those of all worthy poems, focus on love, death, time, the power and perils of the body, the limits and opportunities of language. Inevitably, sadly, yet usefully, they take on sharper and distinctive resonance in the context of their authors' deaths from HIV. Poems must move us, of course, independent of their authors' biographies and fates. But no writer, and no human being, is exempt from the powerful forces that prevail in their times. Wilfred Owen and Paul Celan wrote about the devastating whirlwinds they witnessed during World War I and World War II; the poets in *Persistent Voices*, no matter their subjects, speak to us in the context of AIDS.

Persistent Voices appears at a vital time for poetry and for AIDS. After more than a quarter century of a world epidemic, it is time to garner some perspective about its effect on our lives and literature. And it is important, in a West that too often dismisses HIV disease as a chronic, manageable ailment without great social import or human cost—at least for those with health insurance and good luck—to recall that AIDS has killed and still kills in both hemispheres, depriving us of millions of human lives, as well as the art that those casualties of AIDS could have provided us. It is time to remember the writing of poets we have lost—memorializing and reclaiming those who may not be known to us, and presenting other, more familiar poets within the context of HIV and AIDS.

This anthology is a reminder of poets who didn't write us enough poems. But the book is also, we hope, a heartening tribute. We present it as an appreciation of poets who spoke with arresting power and originality, often in dire circumstances. We present it out of gratitude that their voices do persist, offering us both summons and solace.

Persistent Voices

Steve Abbott

Elegy

The first timepieces were encased in delicate silver skulls.
Momento mori. You may smile to hear this
since much of what we say is gallows humor. We would die laughing
but time encases us both as we are young & healthy.
It was not always so. I recall floating up
from one wrinkled corpse with total delight. It was maybe
the 16th century & I fled into exile to escape the stake.
First goes sight, then hearing, touch, taste & finally smell;
so say the Tibetan monks who wrote their Book of the Dead.
Whether fire, loneliness or love hurts more than death I don't
know but I'm reminded of driving 14 hours to Key West
& lying beside you only to hallucinate your beautiful face
a grinning skull. I lost the poem that told of this.
When I lost my first lover, murdered by an AWOL Marine,
I drove round all night howling helplessly
yet no one could hear me. The windows were up. Before my wife
died, she dreamt of our fishtank breaking & all the fish
flopping into the street. No one would help her save them.
She was a psychologist & fell in love with a psychotic patient,
a kid who wanted to kill everyone in a small town. He was
fantastic in bed. Altho he hated queers he imagined me
coming toward him like Jesus with a garland of roses on my head.
I knew this boded ill fortune.
                              The dead
communicate to us in strange ways, or is it only because it is so

ordinary we think it strange. I don a dark suit & wear a white veil,
pretend I'm a monastery prefect reading the Cloud of Unknowing.
The top of my head floats effortlessly into past or future perfect.
An ancestor of Virginia Woolf, one James Pattle, was put in a
    cask of spirits
when he died & thus shipped back to his wife. She went crazy.
    It's difficult
to conceive what the Black Death mean to 14th century Europe.
    That Hebrew
tribes & Roman Legions massacred whole cities is generally
    forgotten
but then so too Auschwitz. Life is bleak enough
under the best of conditions. I wonder if a book of poems has
    ever
been written about murderers. If not, I'd like to write one.
Caligula, Justinian—one could do volumes on the late Roman
    Emperors alone
But what is more terrible than the death of one child?
The last poem would be about Dan White, the Twinkie killer,
& his love for green Ireland. Its terrible beauty.
When I learned my wife's skull was crushed by a truck, my head
swam like an hourglass into a tv set. All the channels went crazy.
Crickets sounded like Halloween noisemakers & I remember
    explaining the event
to our 2 year old daughter with the aid of her Babar book.
Babar's mother was shot by a mean hunter & that makes Alysia
    sad even now.
We distance ourselves for protection, wear scarves when it's cold.
What seems most outlandish in our autobiography is what really
    happened.

It is only circumstances that make death a terrible event.
She dreamt of our fishtank breaking & all the fish . . .
You should not have to burn your hand every day to feel the
    mystery of fire.

There Is Something to Be Said for Making Love in Lincoln, Nebraska

for Jeff Burling

After ten years' running battle
I have sat down
to smoke the peacepipe
with Nebraska.
A full silence floats
between us (here,
take another toke off the pipe.
Tell me again
of the buffalo you will bring down).

I grew up on this prairie too
like a weed.
The field where I played
cowboys after school
has become a swimming pool
cooling my restlessness.
I can go on walks now

and see where I am going.
I love that clump of girls
on the bridge
not needing to touch them
and I love
the eccentric maples that greet me
when I get off the bus
(even bus rides are more peaceful,
anger too having flattened out
in this spacious state).

At a party I meet you.
We smile.
Our conversation sails adventurously
like a football
between opposite goals.
We sit in the bleachers and cheer.
This is what some men
call love.
And maybe the dancing ghost of Sitting Bull
will bring us together.

Men have taken strange routes
to take root in the land.

To a Soviet Artist in Prison

for Sergei Paradzhanov

They tortured me today
when I created
collage as a degenerate
stance.
I pictured a mountebank mathematician,
his two squinty eyes
wandering on totally different planes,
black on blue
(they kicked me in the ribs for this).
"Zoom 1 plus fat 3
equals zero,"
I wrote under his gaping chin
(for this, they broke my thumbs).
The corners of the poster
        I tore
so it would resemble the State
and I stained it with my own blood
(for this, they hung me by my testicles).

But I was lucky!
When I crawled back to my cell
I found this letter from Karl Shapiro.
"America made me silky, rich and famous,"
        he wrote,
"But I am dying
because no one listens to my words."

Walking This Abandoned Field

Walking this abandoned field I am looking
for something inside myself, an old
shovel perhaps or some evidence of planted seed.
I come upon a tree
much like one I used to climb as a boy
& lying down, my eyes
roam over the frayed hatband of evening sky.

This is how I used to feel loving you.
How sweet the air smelled then, like rain
in Nebraska after a field was plowed.
Now all I can see is this tree
& the memory of how high we once climbed.

Reinaldo Arenas

I Searched for You in the Ancient Night

I searched for you in the eternal night
the same one that devoured Kant and Marco Bruno,
in the sea, and its legendary fury,
in the Bible, and even in popular song.

I must confess that I have dreamed of you
in the confusion of vulgar urinals,
in alleys with their helpless horror,
in a park and in a thousand beaches.

I searched for you, repeating silly things,
looking for a heartbeat in bodies and faces
amid a din of insults and anathemas.

And finally I have found you:
You are solitude.
I kneel in reverence
so I can create my poems.

Translated from the Spanish by Dolores M. Koch

When They Informed Him

When they informed him he was being watched,
that at night when he went out
someone with an extra key searched his room
looked in the medicine cabinet
and in the suspicious manuscripts;
when they informed him that dozens of policemen
were assigned to his case,
that they had bribed his closest relatives,
that his intimate friends
hid their commas and scribblings
in their private parts,
he wasn't scared,
just barely irritated
which he instantly corrected.
He thought: They are not going
to get me to think I am that important.

Translated from the Spanish by Jaime Manrique

The Will to Live Manifests Itself

They're feeding on me:
I feel them crawling all over me, pulling out my nails.
I hear them gnawing my scrotum.
They cover me with sand,
 dancing, dancing on the mound
of sand and stone covering me.
They roll over me and insult me
ranting out loud a deranged judgment against me.
They've buried me.
They have danced on top of me
until the ground was flattened.
They've left, leaving me for dead and buried.
Now I can relax.

El Morro Prison, Havana, 1975

Translated from the Spanish by Jaime Manrique

David Craig Austin

The Fly

As a boy, she ached to cut the wobbly gristle
from between her legs, to walk through the world
no longer the bright spectacle of deceit.

That afternoon the anesthesia swarmed,
the doctors forced thin smiles, as though
losing some brave and imperfect hero;

she knew she'd wake for once concise
and without pain, without the artificial
dramas of false breasts, false skin

plucked hair by hair into gleaming
magnificence. Once, in a darkened theatre,
she wept as The Fly opened its medicine chest

revealing a member floating in a mason jar—
how the creature kept its wand of pale
and useless flesh! Fully healed, she lies

now beneath her handsome new lover who leans,
erect, on the wide heel of his palms, and smiles.
This is what it feels like to be entered.

She hikes the skirt higher, its dyed cloth
between her newborn fingers, and takes
between her teeth its hem like resewn flesh.

The Gifts (*from* "The Farther Branches")

for Lea Baechler

Most of my friends and all of my past
lovers wait for news of one kind or another. Waking
in separate rooms, our breath warms laceworks
of frost. One died four days before Hallowe'en
nearly weightless. I think of metaphors

for marking time: windows, the torn pockets
of winter coats and what falls through, lost
for good. Tomorrow, you leave
for the merciful country, that place where no one
dies (or so I imagine). I don't know

who we meant to be in different lives
though, once, the ground beneath planes seemed
a window we'd learn to fall through, given
the chance. Now, we move through these rooms
slowly, sit by windows and address

the reverberating light outside,
wishing prayer were more than a collection
of beautiful words: *I am poured out*
like water ... Once, in a graveyard north
of Pittsburgh, we stood before

a cinder block chapel with smoke-
glass doors and Jesus fixed to the outside wall;
Mary looked up from his terrible feet
to his stainless steel ribs, thin as the blades
of pocket knives. It wasn't pity written

on her face. I want to tell you
that I'm dying, I don't know who we'll be
when you return, or if January will hold together
the bones of need. Last winter, you carried me
north on Seventh Avenue,

my arms around your shoulders and my legs
around your waist, the two of us drunk enough
to wake in a movie house where the gorgeous
fucked on screen and the desperate between reels.
And none can keep alive his own

soul ... Out of grief comes rage,
as, years ago, I watched the power lines
around my father's house burn, flames
shot through with blue electric sustenance.
I stood on the lawn and waited for the danger

to pass. The danger never once
came close enough, until now. This morning,
after waking enough for the world,
I walked the markets of Hell's Kitchen,
gathering our dinner. Home again

and short of breath, I climb the stairs,
reach for the door as though for grace.
The stock boils now, a landscape of fervent air.
The sliced flesh of vegetables goes into the pot
and we wait. Once more, the bare December

trees beneath this window bend,
their living branches greet one another
and bend. Tonight, we'll bow our heads
over steaming bowls of late abundance,
whisper our separate graces for the living, the dead—

blessed, the gifts we receive.

The Music of God Walking Away

for Joan Lunoe

My Spanish neighbor leans
into the airshaft, pulling back the day's
clothes from a length of wire and two rusting
pulleys. Watching the laundry disappear,
I step out of the shower in my kitchen, light
one of the two working burners on my circa-1957
gas stove. We live on the last floor
before the roof. At night, there are footsteps
overhead, not tenants but men from the street,
their plodding the music of God
walking away. The door's unlocked, they come
and go at will. Our visitors must know
He won't ever return. Some mornings,
they hold one another for company or warmth,
hold trash bags full of empty soda cans.

After dark, the first lightning,
the thin music of a transistor radio
rises from an apartment downstairs, the rasp
of what must be either *Shut up!* or *Go to sleep*
in Dominican. Rain; no rain. The barbed wire
on the roof rattles like the ankle bells
of Indian dancers. I walk five flights
to the street, leaving a foreign language
for the barking of dogs, Smokey Robinson
and the Miracles' *You've Really Got a Hold on Me,*

the lumbering drone of cars. Blessed
by the verdant fingers of Mexican bean trees,
we know of no other place to call home.

A Perfectible Curse

for Robin Nemlich

I.

All night, the sirens interrupt those lovers sleeping
peacefully or not, the consequence

of choosing life in this city, country, year—
gothic and spectacular as flame.

The end of January. The longest night returns
with each new change in temperature.

We huddle afternoons in cafes and bus shelters,
waiting for the weather's passage,

the expected miracle we might or might not deserve—
or less, for the leather of our shoes to dry.

II.

All over town, the buildings rise
the way we learn to sleep, sometimes badly

and with regrets. The cranes lean from rooftops
like hands curled to hold the sky. Tonight,

fire burned through a warehouse near the river,
mailing smoke and ash to other tenements.

For hours, you could see the distant neighbors
on their roofs, stamping out the cinders

falling around them like confetti.

Thomas Avena

Cancer Garden

The cancer garden, protected by buildings, one unfinished. Still
the wind will continue through the garden when these walls
are sewn in. Everything known in the cancer garden devolves
to breath. If we can, we open gray chambers and fingers
of the lung. Such breath can sting. Here are vermilion
snapdragons, mild blue agapanthus, poppy. Here in our
veins is the blood of the Madagascar periwinkle; its sulfates—
vincristine, vinblastine, *effective against neoplasm.*

In the garden we find the man whose veins collapsed nine
times, and each time the neon-colored serum stopped.
The technicians tried their tricks to open a vein,
and the strange, ambivalent poison stained (oh
how to make these poisons more selective—more
devious and therefore purposeful). In the cancer
garden we are grateful for the slenderness of needles,
the wisdom of the phlebotomist's hand. For the plain
explanation of a doctor—what is known, and what is

unknown. In the garden there is breath, ambivalence
(in the sense of unknowing—can you live with the fall
of water on your brow, drop by drop). Can you live
with the chill, with bright daubs of petal-bruised flesh,
catheter under the skin. You can look at your body

naked in a mirror, with your hands you can defend
its territories. Is the cancer sinister or blameless? Or

just cells, like all life, with a blind and blinding purpose.
An instinct to survive. In the garden, imagine cancer
as weak and depressed. If the cancer is acid, then the soil
of your body is alkaline; if alkaline, then acid. Let us
pray your body inhospitable to it. Your assertion greater
than that of the cancer—your desire to live so much the
greater. A riot of marigolds shooting up the spine—a firework

of neutrophil. In the cancer garden all the creatures are active.
Every day, a thousand kindnesses, or a thousand suspicions,
hyper-real, like the furniture of the infusion clinic. In
the cancer garden all of nature is laughing.

for the inauguration of the Mt. Zion Cancer Center Garden

Plums (1989)

Karen brings plums
from her garden—
fallen
or ripened on the tree,
bird pecked; all
go into the same brown bag.

For years she has brought
these fragrant or sodden
gifts of fruit

as though a sackful
of softly oozing plums
could save us from
despair;

all harvest summer they come . . .

plums in the estuary
roiling

plums like small sacred organs
removed

in Sumeria
a violation of plums
the sweet, dully thudding avalanche

and whether we eat them
or not
             they putrefy

To the Artist Dying Young

Disease has its own
motion, doesn't
it – the implacable
motion of a glacier
and its indifference
to your will

don't be deceived as if I had no
more force
than a whisper

or something already dead

I want you to fight
the bastards

now black eyes
push with fever
from the devoured face

you are a skein
of bones un-

raveling:
vapor and
lymph

light as champagne

*

in the dusty
sour-milk scented room
you select colors—
a streak of primary yellow

blisters

daub in gray,
in black . . .
color becomes unbearable

*

it is the slowest dance:
you didn't choose your partner
with his gray hood
or his sardonic
joker's face

yet gracefully he draws you

and when you
stumble
he comforts you with
an iron grip

(he is not the suave
lady dressed in black
who exits through a mirror)

Charles Barber

Prose Poem

But no, the palm trees had no reply. Clifford searched the beach, of course a sea of garbage. A real anachronism, a sweatshirt in Florida: still, babies huddled by the outdoor pool, scarily close to the golf course, upending their blue drinks or squeezing into the hot tub. At night, the family pushed little letters around the Scrabble board, sending each other furtive messages disguised as simple squares, emotional Chiclets. The sky yielded not one inch though he begged for its friendship. Here and there carts darted among the bushes. Oldsters laughed, was it "gaily"? Security was tight. The project to chase down some herons for their sperm to make AZT came to naught when a dispatch in the form of the *Times* informed them it was herrings, not herons, that they should be seducing. Where, oh where, are there herrings on a golf course? Mary preferred flamingoes anyway she said. Everywhere, too much food. Bicycling in the Ding Darling Bird Preserve cleared their heads, until numerous alligators stared challengingly. "Mom, Mom," he cried out, but it was the Gulf Coast. Land mines would have helped. Strangely, the landscape was void of teens, all the skins wrinkled or new; perhaps a terrible blight? Cliff would have to search for the teens. There are teens on golf courses, a childhood lesson learned hard and fast. But pleasure had made him languid, a kind of sunny poison. There was no hardship. Still, the house shook on the moorings. Still, the Scrabble letters slid dangerously this way and that. Still, the rain fell.

Thirteen Things About a Catheter

White tube
In cephalic vein;
To the right atrium
Of the heart (see illustration):
Access.

A cuff,
Made of dacron,
Serves as a barrier
To infections, tunneled under
The skin.

Daily
I tend its bud,
Swabbing away the dust,
The slugs of dirt that in the night
Advance.

The nurse
Is called Bud, too:
A gay man, but grumpy;
Won't use my towels, asks "don't you have . . .
Paper?"

A fish,
Hung from the pole,
Striped with words of caution:
"To expire in ninety-one"
(Like me?)

The bag
Bloated with drug,
Takes the hook at line's end;
Hopeful and still, I reel it in,
Dripping . . .

Detached,
Or pulled apart,
Silently blood spurts out;
I stare at it uncaringly,
Unmoved.

Or sex:
A white T-shirt
Discreetly veils the thing.
Between us, while locked together,
It hurts.

Bandaged,
Walking wounded,
The cap beneath my shirt
Signals to other veterans:
"Soldier."

A kite,
Flapping skyward,
Dreaming only of the ground,
While dirty hands keep the string tight,
Tired.

Or Mom
With aging son,
Feeds from her third nipple,
Thinks: "Please won't you go away soon,
Dear one."

The dream.
Finally well,
Over me lies his arm;
The hole in my chest a lip-smudge,
Stamped, sealed.

Grotesque,
Life-supporting,
Deforming and healing;
Not a cure; insistent I be
Life-like.

What Was Said

Love said,
The garden is coolest   in the morning
See where the deer have not eaten   the stone lion speaks

Dismay said
How has this happened   to me   what did I do   where has it
        come from
                        go away

Illness said,
Now you will wait beyond all suffering   suffer beyond all knowing
Small moments   will not exist   only the large hand unfolding
        and folding

Childhood said,
The cars the Tonka Toy cars   they carry me small as Stuart Little
        home over the hill

The table by the window said,
The lamp   the lake   the bowl of peonies   the pad and pen
        Now evening comes

Remorse said,
It was the golden ball   hanging over the pool table
            shimmering beckoning
            turning slow as futility

Hopefulness said,
Red will be there   the red-curtained theatre   the plate of
          red beets
          the red-faced mailman at noon

The friend said,
Meanings collapse   we go along   variously lost   dinner done
          repeating stories

Old age said,
I kick   I cry   put down the cup   find in the basement
          parking lot
          the car marked "rest"

Dying, I said,
I am the preyed upon   I stand in line   shuffling   uneasy
          marked
          the sun   a disappointment   small   pale
          locating no one as it arches into airlessness.

William Barber

Cancer (*from* "The Zodiac Poems")

In this wet weather
my mother is weeping
for the old stage at Shavertown
where for a dollar
she would play a white piano
and sing
       the black velvet songs
of the war years.
In her home now
the kitchen is
immaculate.
She comes down the long hall stairs
quietly,

and it is only her small heels
on the wooden steps
that sing.

Coming of Age

They raised the rent
on our house
by the roadside.

My liver is exhausted
with cheap wine,

and thou
hating this poverty
hast split.

Simple pleasures too
are disillusioning.

O give me a yacht
on the rolling sea
a million dollars
and thou. And thou.

Hustler Joe

Joe is going back to Arkansas,
says it's "on account" his Dad's sick,
and his brother has a job building boats
and drives a Cougar. At the hotel,
Joe paid his bill by selling sections
of his pink flesh to San Francisco
on the wide meat highway. Said it was
a pain in the ass. "Course, so's the war"
he said, preferring women. Yet old Joe
really gave a man his money's worth;
he'd roll either way, fag fucking, nothing to it
but a little hurting, nothing to a mouthful
of hot jizz, even an old man's jizz,
so long he's paying.

We was buddies, me and Joe.
I'd screw him before he'd go out,
just to get him loose, for his consumers.
At night, sometimes, he'd blow me
if the lights were out. Such a pretty face,
real blond hair, marine cut, the "shits"
and "jesuses" completely natural. Ten dollars
hid in the bible, six in his pocket, on the prowl.
Joe walked through rain like it wasn't raining,
looked at a green wall and a torn shade
and saw only his thoughts, beer, broads, the open road.

Tomorrow morning he'll take the Greyhound
to Fayetteville, the Ozark mountains. They said

$44.25 for a one way ticket. I gave him ten dollars
for a ride on his back, dreaming of horses
on the green slopes of Appalachia, but
he was still $25 short. He pulled up his pants
and we said goodbye, forever I guess,
and he was back on the street in his blue snugs
with his big smile, so available. If interested,
please write to this poem, care of the wind,
because by now Joe's been gone so long
he's fathered his own kids in Arkansas.

Virgo (*from* "The Zodiac Poems")

You have sliced
through the thin skin
of the tomato

the knife is
poised in
your hand

You have prepared an oil
for these perfect slices,

now you bring them
on a small china plate
to the table.

And you have
embroidered your long gown
with paisley, saying,

> "Tonight I will let you
> come to me
> in my small bed."

Walta Borawski

Invisible History

My shrink told me it was unnatural to be
obsessed with the Nazi extermination of
homosexuals   Look at me I'm normal he

said I sleep nights & I'm healthy enough
to listen to your stories & others worse than
yours & I still have sex & *I'm* Jewish so

what's with these nightmare pogroms   find
yourself a hot guy to go to bed with or
do it on the floor of his car but

stop it with these death camps. I
knew he was right, that his people had
lost millions more than my   people, but

piles of emaciated   tortured   worked-to-
death   gassed-to-death   clubbed-to-death
bodies   resemble each other   & they

resemble *us*   Look at that man on top
of the others   Look at his beard   He
could be me. When I was six my

father first told me about liberation
of the camps   by the Allies   he was
US Army & they entered at

last & those bodies, he said   those bodies.
By time I was 15 my eye doctor showed
mercy to me put me on sleeping pills

Circles around my eyes   I told him I
couldn't sleep & when I did fall I
found myself behind wire—barbed,

or electric: my head shaved   an empty
expression leering back at me   at every-
one in this odd century of horror

so systematic so organized. I'll give you
these pills he said   But don't abuse them
& cut out the fantasies, you're not even

Jewish

(No title)

English was only a second
language, never second nature
to my maternal grandfather   He

would shout the heavy
fragments of sentence:
Money! Under! Mattress!

He didn't trust banks, he
knew that here in America
we hide things. When I

was 15 he wanted to see me
with my pants down   I took
them   off   in his toolshed

He ran his fingertips across
my pubic hair & said
Ah! Moustache! That year

he died & I began
looking for other men who'd
take his sort of interest

but it's never been the same
with proper sentences.

Things Are Still Sudden & Wonderful

Once it was 1962 & somebody
kissed you you freaked he

held you down pressed his
15-yr.-old football team thighs   hard

against yr. thin-kid-with-glasses
legs   It was like a Lana Turner movie

; you decided to be gay. In 1982 yr. lover
puts you down on all fours & masturbates

you sometimes you come with a leash on
in more than one room. You've

not forgotten the football player's name

Traveling in the Wrong Century

for Joan Doyle

Hotels we stay in
have no flowers left by management,
we manage without
writing tables set discreetly
off-lobby; no chandeliers
cast dancing rainbows 'cross
our faces as our feet
take rich baby steps
into deep carpet. There are no
potted palms, no old world
charm, no bell boys, damn
near no fantasy. If shoes
are left in the hall they're
polished off by morning.

Trying to Write a Love Poem

for M. Bronski

Since most of my words go to describe
loves that fail, tricks who come & go,
it's no surprise I have no poems for you.

Shall I, trying to write one, say: You
are the man who stole white lilacs from
Harvard to help me find spring in a

dull season? Or that three years ago we
met in a bath house in New York City, strangers
making love in the shelter of sauna & steam?

Would it be too silly to say I like to think
we're Leonard & Virginia Woolf? Don't worry—
I'll not tell which of us is Virginia. But

if I suffer a total breakdown after trying
to write you this poem—& if you
drop all work on your next essay to

put me together, take care of my cat, they'll
know. Meanwhile, *you* should know that
when I see aged couples clutching each

other, walking quick as they can from
muggers & death—I see us. & that if you
die first, someone will have to, like they

would a cat without hope or home, put me to
as it's sometimes called, sleep; & though you
don't believe in heaven, & taught me how empty

& odd my own plan for it was, I imagine we've
already known it—at the baths, in your
loft bed; in stolen lilacs, in each stroke you

give my cat, my cock; & though I'm agnostic
now, I never question why the archangel who
sent down the devil is called Saint Michael.

William Bory

Alarum

The window shades come down.
        The sun drops his penny in the
            cup of days.
All along the waterfront, the joggers
            lean on their elbows.

The boys at home
        in their sweatshirts
close their eyes and breathe deeply,
        thinking of the laurels
            that wreathe their brows
               in fantasy.

You cannot surpass them for . . .

In the finished basements
            of a hundred suburbs,
        they hump the ottoman,
        thinking of their babies.
After it's over, they look corny,
        their mouths half open
        at the tits of sleep.

You cannot imagine how . . .

The joy we feel is joy we steal,
       time races under heaven.
Up then, lads, and get your fill,
       for it's already evening.

Early Masses

Where the dark soil fumes
       beneath the vines,
   amid the bright-capped trulli,
   and the furry pines crouch
       over the rough-hewn wall,
the poppies, in their early masses,
   recall our savior's blood,
   the fall of slaughtered heroes,
   and the flood of history books.
How innocent they look,
   these shiny flowers, drenched in dew,
   flourishing for their brief
   and sanguine hour.

I am ignorant of botany,
   these flowers tell me what I have to know.
They don't know their names either;
   they only bloom and blow.

I am ignorant of geology,
    these stones inform me of what I have to say.
Gneiss, mica, chalk, clay,
    all teach silence in a different way.

I am ignorant of theology,
    yet, I can see, religion leaves her empty
        place to poetry.

On Seeing Farmboys in Church

In white shirts, in white churches,
                the farmboys are asleep.
Their tow heads nod beneath the slumberous ponder
                of the murmured sermon.

Now they are dreaming, of turning potatoes
                out of their cold beds,
        of breaking the ice with their heels
                on winter mornings,
            of hamburgers and snowmobiles.

What is J.C. to them, but a boy
                they wouldn't like at school?

Their brown limbs stir beneath the starched cloth.
Each heart beats its wings like an excited bird,
   and, with no thought of wings, hearts,
   heavens or hells, their melodious yawns
      make part song.

Their days full of sowings and scraps, moonings
      and crops, as errant and regular
    as the seasons,
      mark off the preacher's periods.

Sea, that washes this great ball
    with your eternal ebb and tide,
    careful housewife who keeps
    this lustre shining,
to think that they may never see you,
who, today, sit dreaming in this old white church,
    so far from your blue hems.

Joe Brainard

1970

1970
is a good year
if for no other reason
than just because
I'm tired of complaining.

Selections from *I Remember*

I remember Liberace.

I remember "Liberace loafers" with tassels.

I remember those bright-colored nylon seersucker shirts that you could see through.

I remember many first days of school. And that empty feeling.

I remember the clock from three to three-thirty.

I remember when girls wore cardigan sweaters backwards.

I remember when girls wore lots of can-can slips. It got so bad (so noisy) that the principal had to put a limit on how many could be worn. I believe the limit was three.

I remember thin gold chains with one little pearl hanging from them.

I remember mustard seed necklaces with a mustard seed inside a little glass ball.

I remember pony tails.

I remember when hoody boys wore their blue jeans so low that the principal had to put a limit on that too. I believe it was three inches below the navel.

I remember shirt collars turned up in back.

I remember Perry Como shirts. And Perry Como sweaters.

I remember duck-tails.

I remember Cherokee haircuts.

I remember no belts.

I remember many Sunday afternoon dinners of fried chicken or pot roast.

I remember my first oil painting. It was of a chartreuse green field of grass with a little Italian village far away.

I remember when I tried out to be a cheerleader and didn't make it.

I remember many Septembers.

I remember one day in gym class when my name was called out I just couldn't say "here." I stuttered so badly that sometimes words just wouldn't come out of my mouth at all. I had to run around the field many times.

I remember a rather horsy-looking girl who tried to seduce me on a New York City roof. Although I got it up, I really didn't want to do anything, so I told her that I had a headache.

I remember one football player who wore very tight faded blue jeans, and the way he filled them.

I remember when I got drafted and had to go way downtown to take my physical. It was early in the morning. I had an egg for breakfast and I could feel it sitting there in my stomach. After roll call a man looked at me and ordered me to a different line than most of the boys were lined up at. (I had very long hair which was more unusual then than it is now.) The line I was sent to turned out to be the line to see the head doctor. (I was going to ask to see him anyway.) The doctor asked me if I was queer and I said yes. Then he asked me what homosexual experiences I had had and I said none. (It was the truth.) And he believed me. I didn't even have to take my clothes off.

I remember a boy who told me a dirty pickle joke. It was the first clue I had as to what sex was all about.

I remember when my father would say "Keep your hands out from under the covers" as he said goodnight. But he said it in a nice way.

I remember when I thought that if you did anything bad, policemen would put you in jail.

I remember one very cold and black night on the beach alone with Frank O'Hara. He ran into the ocean naked and it scared me to death.

I remember lightning.

I remember wild red poppies in Italy.

I remember selling blood every three months on Second Avenue.

I remember a boy I once made love with and after it was all over he asked me if I believed in God.

*

I remember orange icing on cupcakes at school Halloween parties.

I remember autumn.

I remember walking home from school through the leaves alongside the curb.

I remember jumping into piles of leaves and the dust, or whatever it is, that rises.

I remember raking leaves but I don't remember burning leaves. I don't remember what we "did" with them.

I remember "Indian Summer." And for years not knowing what it meant, except that I figured it had something to do with Indians.

I remember exactly how I visualized the Pilgrims and the Indians having the first Thanksgiving dinner together. (Very jolly!)

I remember Jack Frost. Pumpkin pie. Gourds. And very blue skies.

I remember Halloween.

I remember usually getting dressed up as a hobo or a ghost. One year I was a skeleton.

I remember one house that always gave you a dime and several houses that gave you five-cent candy bars.

I remember after Halloween my brother and me spreading all our loot out and doing some trading.

I remember always at the bottom of the bag lots of dirty pieces of candy corn.

I remember the smell (not very good) of burning pumpkin meat inside jack-o'-lanterns.

I remember orange and black jellybeans at Halloween. And pastel-colored ones for Easter.

I remember "hard" Christmas candy. Especially the ones with flower designs. I remember not liking the ones with jelly in the middle very much.

I remember some beautiful German Christmas tree ornaments in the shape of birds and houses and people.

I remember the dangers of angel hair.

I remember having my Christmas shopping list all made out before December.

I remember the fear of not getting a present for someone who might give me one.

I remember after Christmas shopping coming home and gloating over everything I bought.

I remember Rosemary Clooney and Bing Crosby and "I'm Dreaming of a White Christmas."

I remember how sad and happy at the same time Christmas carols always made me feel: all warm inside.

I remember seeing every year that movie about "Macy's" and "Gimbel's" and the old man who thought he was Santa Claus.

I remember, after Christmas caroling, hot chocolate.

I remember buying a small bottle of Chanel No. 5 for my mother for Christmas one year but when I told my father how much it cost I had to take it back.

I remember not being able to fall asleep Christmas Eve.

I remember more than once leaving the price tag on a present.

I remember very clearly (visually) a bride doll sitting in a red wagon under the Christmas tree when I was very young. (For me.)

I remember opening my first packages very fast and my last few very slowly.

I remember after opening packages what an empty day Christmas day is.

I remember Linda Berg. She confided in me once, though she wouldn't "go very far," she really dug having her breasts played with (which, to me, was going pretty far) and did I think it was wrong? (Help!)

I remember a "white trash" boy with an enormously tall crew cut long after crew cuts were in.

I remember pulling the elastic band of my underwear down behind my balls, which gives your whole sex an "up-lift," which makes you look like you've got more down there than you really do.

I remember the fear of—what if all of a sudden out in the middle of public somewhere you get a hard-on?

I remember sex on too much grass and the total separation of my head from what's going on down there.

I remember when everything is going along just swell ("pant-pant") and then all of a sudden neither one of you knows for sure what to "do" next. (Mutual hesitation.) That if not acted upon quickly can be a real, pardon the pun, "downer."

I remember, after a lot of necking, how untheatrical the act of getting undressed can sometimes be.

I remember, in the heart of passion once, trying to get a guy's turtle-neck sweater off. But it turned out not to be a turtle-neck sweater.

I remember a sex fantasy sequence in my head of being forced to "perform" on the floor, under the stairs, of an apartment building I either lived in, or was visiting, I can't remember which. Needless to say, the mad sex fiend criminal rapist was pretty cute to boot.

I remember, with the one you love, familiar gestures that can drive you up the wall.

I remember a small top drawer full of nylons , and my mother, in a rush, trying to find two that matched.

I remember finding things in that drawer I wasn't supposed to see, smothered in nylons.

I remember the olive green velvet lining of my mother's olive green "leather" jewelry box, with fold-out trays. When alone in the house, I loved going through it, examining each piece carefully, trying to pick out my favorites. And sometimes, trying on something, but mostly, I just liked to look.

I remember learning very early in life the art of putting back everything exactly the way it was.

I remember affectionate squeezes in public from my father. Usually of a joke-strangle sort. And not knowing how to respond. So I'd turn red, with a big grin on my face, and look down until it was all over with.

I remember how difficult it is to let a "public" grin fall gracefully.

I remember catching myself with an expression on my face that doesn't relate to what's going on anymore.

I remember practicing flexing my jaw muscles, because I thought it looked sexy.

I remember, when my eyebrows began to spread over my nose bridge, thinking it might make me look a bit more like Montgomery Clift. (A bit *more*?) Yes—I just remembered—I did have a period of secretly thinking I slightly resembled Montgomery Clift.

Sick Art

Mona Lisa's smile often causes observers to overlook the fact that she has no eyebrows.

One skin specialist offered the suggestion that Leonardo da Vinci's model was suffering from a skin disease called alopecia. Alopecia is a skin disease in which one has no eyebrows.

On the other hand, many women in those days shaved their eyebrows and Leonardo da Vinci's model may have just been following the fad.

There is no doubt, however, that Rodin's *The Thinker* has bunions on both feet.

Today, with modern art, it is not so easy to spot diseases and physical disorders.

Many doctors, however, have noticed a strong relationship between various skin diseases and the paintings of Jackson Pollock.

Fungus infections are very common in the art of the Middle Ages and Renaissance.

Donald Britton

Hart Crane Saved from Drowning (Isle of Pines, 1926)

He stood a long time while U.S.S. Milwaukee
oxidized at the salt-wash pier. The succulent
hot stiletto beach pitched his nerves like waves
and waves bombed thunder cloud to palm.

A dolphin materialized drilling
through serrated foam. Bacardi and fifteen-cent
Corona-Coronas slaked his thirst for sailors
now: he puked in volleys on ignited sand.

Fish-eye, coruscated scales of surf, the bird
with a note Rimbaud speaks of as "making you blush"—
coral negatives plashed gold and azure plaster
in the harbor: death could come like a blackout drunk.

But the naked Cubano all testicles and rod
laving amid ripe tendrils of the water ridges
trumped fate with desire; so he postponed his resolve
for six years and a boat and a woman.

Notes on the Articulation of Time

It becomes a critical account
of all that's spoken, done:
the drawing in of breaths, even,
these nights whose atmosphere
reminds us of mountains,
white volumes of air. We need

these narratives, we want them:
the city lies before us
and some one person in the sleeve
of a streetlamp awaits
our enraptured attention
as we await the concept of the city

which tells us how we move
in the parti-colored geographies
about us. We can't be certain
we are moving toward this person
nor do we require certitude.
It is enough to acknowledge

the movement itself, shavings
of light inscribing a circle.
Our childlike sense of the other
bears these forces toward
completion and renewal,
a lexis of infatuated sounds.

Sonnet (*from* "Four Poems")

My unkempt mind is yours, and the purity
Of my body, and the lesions joining them.
My outfit is yours, though you wear
But one thing, amply clothed in the capsule
Of a single sense of yourself. You tire
Of our games. I never tire
Of them or you or the feelings that correspond
To our being together in this neutral climate.
Our natures are cold but for love
Dreadfully radiant in us. Emptiness abounds.

The conch bears no sea sounds, only the silence
Of a wave's interior calm. I think of you
And light breaks over still water. Already
You are forgetting this: the day, the hour,
The primary colors.

Zona Temperata

I may see on my wall
a street of Paris, by Utrillo,
where black figures walk,
as I walk, in the evenings
past houses walled by white stone;
each house has a
garden and trellis and
shuttered windows. On the wall
in my room is
a suburb street of Paris,
painted by Utrillo,
le vierge, le vivace, et le bel aujhourd'hui.

The work of Utrillo
   presents the common streets: rooftops
          and doorways and pavement.
          There are sometimes trees.
   One can imagine life on those streets
      as their residents know it,
here on the wall of my room.
   In the street below my window
the gutters are clogged by leaves
and grass and branches
clipped by the wind. The glass of my
window is thin.

   A street of Paris, done by Utrillo,
   hangs on the wall in my room.

Gil Cuadros

The Breath of God That Brings Life

for K.M. with devotion

> . . . Saying it then,
> against what comes: *wife*,
> while I can, while my breath,
> each hurried petal
> can still find her.
> w—RAYMOND CARVER

The heels of Kevin's palms massage my back
guide my head upward till I watch the ceiling.
It feels as if my bones could snap as twigs
the loss of spirit, the loss of breath,
but faith I put in my lover's hands,w
his strength not to show fear when I am fearful.
Folded over a chair, ribbed oak
against my chest, I am lungs newly cleared
the process of gallium, infusions, respite.
Up close tiny fissures run across the grain.
I moan.

It's Friday, his bedroom, the first real rain,
the sound of the orchard, the garden,
drops on thick green leaves

avocados, plums, the more delicate grapefruit.
Inside, water seeps along the slatted windows,
a rivulet forms, stains gray the walls.
Kevin kneads between neck and shoulders,
thumbs roll down the spine like furrows.
I give in to his pressure, tension released.
His face gives nothing away but the job at hand,
small victories we've coaxed from my body,
a garden he has worked during war.
Again I moan.
He asks, "Did you say something?"

"Past the trees, can you hear it?"
                                        A man is in the rain,
"... *alluhu akbar, laillaha illala* ..."
a muezzin calls noon prayer,
Kevin repeats the rhymes of his words,
says this day, this hour is Jumma.
He offers a crisp, blue Qur'an,
gold leaf pressed into leather, a flower.
I cherish its weight with free hands

and struggle for more air, chest held for a long moment
as if I had a lot to say,
"Honey."
Remember when I could not just a week ago
inhale fully,
birch leaf, golden seal tea.
Now I explode, muscles surrender to peace,
Kevin's flushed palms,

recall a dead man's poem
a wedding vow made of simple things:
water,
prayer,
breath.

There Are Places You Don't Walk at Night, Alone

1.

Whittier Blvd., Beverly, Atlantic,
over by Johnson's Market,
or the Projects on Brooklyn.
There weren't any Bloods
or Crips yet on TV and everyone
bought bandannas
at Sav-on. Combinations
of blue and red packages,
the cellophane crinkled in the hand.
I wore them quartered
in my back pocket,
loose as a hanky.
The *cholos* pulled wool
beanies low,
just above their eyes,
warm and brown.
They'd cuff me from behind,

their hands lingering on my neck, saying
"Come here faggot, kiss me."
Their shoes made me crawl,
black mirrors, pointed tips,
Imperials that my lips fell upon
and leather soles
that brushed the hair out of my face
nearly blinding me.

2.

Manzanita, Hoover, Del Mar,
The Detour's After Hours.
I told him you had to walk
with an attitude.
Leather isn't thick enough
for a Buck knife
or a Corona
bottle, its end
jagged, twisted into
a washboard stomach.
Marc's t-shirt turned red,
the paramedics wouldn't touch him.
I filled in the holes,
my fingers adding pressure
on a hunter-green bandanna.
It changed to black,
warm in my hands
His eyes were open,
his face rolled in my lap.

3.

Marengo, Arroyo, Colorado.
I walk like a policeman
to the bus bench
and some homeboys are waiting.
One has his shirt off
and his tattoo back reads,
"Viva La Raza."
They notice the fags going
into the white glass door
of the Adult Books and Films.
They see the pale limbs extended,
the shallow cheeks spotted,
the pink bandannas folded like
their own blue. They want to go in
but they're afraid they'd bleed.
The one-eighty rolls up
and they sit together
knees touching
corduroy against Levi's.
Brilliantine falls from their hair,
Three Roses, onto the hot vinyl seats.
My leather jacket creaks.
I want to smash them into the windows,
make them spread their legs,
my boots kicking them wide,
let my spit drip
into their ears,
seep into their brains,
tell them how much I love them.

To the First Time

As if everything special was marked holiday,
the cold night air made strange
by mask and costume, hoof and sequin.
A feast day on Santa Monica Boulevard,
drag on Halloween. Voices crowded the corners,
bustle to bustle and I was still a virgin watching
nervous-eyed, the bare-chested men act out Pan.

Even his name was exotic, Emerson, Southern
in root, a loose drawl. I admired his tongue.
We stood in the Revolver's door-frame,
the bar pumped up like a heart over-burdened
and in his blue suit he conveyed ease.
It was easy to hand over innocence,
all it took was him asking.
I could have fallen there already, his chin's bristle,
the bite of his teeth, his lips, autumn's chapped effect.
He laid it all on the bed's head table, alongside candles,
incense burners, the Welch's and vodka in tumblers.
His patience, the fingers lubricating parts of my body
I denied existed, kept under wrap by briefs and jeans.
When he told me to turn over, I did, trusted
his chest on my back, his legs separating mine,
winced at the pressure of pain.
It's rare, he said later, to be able to do it the first time,
to allow the muscles to relax and accept this pleasure.
A ragged towel on his lap, a swirl of jism
hooked inside a hair's curl, his thigh damp from himself.
He wanted to protect me from the things out there,

ready to hurt, hands explaining, pointed at the white paste,
a danger already prevalent, my desire to dab it on a finger
when he turned, to swallow the treat,
my belief, love could never be harmful,
that nights would last forever.

Sam D'Allesandro

After Being Wanted

You eat through me a wound,
in one night to the cold bones,
until desire is finished using me
up—like a death.

The tender fingers that spoke so quietly
back and forth across my belly,
the mouth searching and blind
around my frozen neck,
are now all silent and gone.

The sound of water in the hall bathroom
is clear as you wash away
my imprint like a smudge.
Almost anonymous footsteps
quietly find their way out.

Alone, moments
after being wanted
I sit and smoke in the wrinkled bed,
the sheets still shy
and smelling of us.

In Paris

In Paris I have hepatitis,
while Nanci scours the museums
and yells at old french men
who make passes on the street,
bringing me home fauvist reproductions
as my skin grows zebric and faded.

Tired feet continue through the thick summer
the french find so insulting to grace:
I can hear the older and poorer *mesdames*
trudging along the narrow Rue de Charmaine
in black dresses, carrying bags,
skinny bread poking from the top

like spikes, like fat-bladed pitchforks,
like the weapons of their trade.
The air from the courtyard window is full
with foreign sounds, scents of drying laundry,
and outside the cars fight
as they try to round the Bastille.

In Paris Nanci walks, coming home tired
to tell me what she's seen and read as I watch
her concentration in the dim gaslight—
before I fade out, lids resting,
before I must run to the bowl again, unable
to hold down even water for long.

I am drowning in a sickness I pretend exotic,
like Gide's, and I laugh at my own stupidity
while getting so thin I will soon disappear
beneath the buzzing of the room's silence.
I think of dying in this crumbling
house with the tall windows . . .

If I must I don't mind,
at least the daylight is good,
making soft shadows on the plaster, dancing
patterns of distortion from the leaded glass—
like me, too thick and unstable
for anything to pass through unaltered.

Nanci says when I'm better
she'll take me to Spain
where once we ate *paella*, full
of drunkenness and happy every night . . .
The blue Mediterranean where germans
slather oil on plaster-white skin

and the shower water is too hard
to make soap lather.
She counts the days and I make her promise
to bury me in Rome, where sheep
keep the graveyard mowed,
grazing softly overhead.

Slippery Sin

You sank six stone feet
into the starched snow bed,
your stomach pumped and drained
right down to the thirsty hole
of your sore and fitful soul.

Little groans wrap your throat
with a thin-voiced scarf
made to drain the pain.
You turn away eyeless, sick
at finding yourself still lunged.

Tubes suck at your arm
like hungry snakes or a rape
forcing the unwanted inside.
We are both ashamed
of your failure.

I'm leaving, I've lost my ability
for suicide. What made you think
you'd catch that prize?
Damn you for reminding me
what a hard animal it is to track.

Freshly cut and fallen,
talked back into living, I know
you will try to die again:

white knuckled and clutching,
praying this time it will all seep out,

but oh what a slippery, slippery sin
trying to do God's work for him.

Tory Dent

Clash

As if without agony the white convertible, a Mustang, peels
    along,
pierces the chiffon-thin dawn, sheet by sheet,
white as white chocolate or a snow leopard's spots.

Far off people make love and moan as if in great pain,
but they're not, through their pleasure be pitched at an
    undetectable level
like a whistle only dogs can hear.

And I, as if a dog, hear it all,
hued yet whole in its spectrum, a hologram Xeroxed to perfection
where the exaction of exhaust exhalation and heaves of passion
stack this cruel world upon its cruelty.
Their secretions smear their loins like white chocolate,
and from their eyes spurt white tears of pity.

I both watch and want to stop
the lovemaking bodies that wriggle with self-centered abandon
deep inside my body the way a dream does or hope will despite
    my cynicism;
pulling me to move by collar and chain
within my emotionlessness, motionless as a parked car,
a white convertible, a snow leopard devoured by dogs,
I both watch and want to stop.

Immigrant in My Own Life

for Marie Ponsot

Broken dreams hovering like the shadow of a branch—
How, I wonder, do I begin again?
With resistance I read back over my old poems
Trying to understand what it is that has been.

How, I wonder, do I begin again?
Nothing looks familiar, no matter where I look.
Trying to understand what it is that has been;
Foreign sky, foreign street, foreign trees with their foreign leaves.

Nothing looks familiar, no matter where I look:
I don't know my name, what I am without disease.
Foreign sky, foreign street, foreign trees with their foreign leaves.
Foreign tears my eyes won't always for me make.

I don't know my name, what I am without disease.
Help me remember, help me imagine or just desire again.
Foreign tears my eyes won't always for me make,
Come back to me whoever, wherever you've been.

Help me remember, help me imagine or just desire again.
For seventeen years I've waited like a soldier's wife for something.
Come back to me whoever, wherever you've been.
For seventeen years I've said "I won't live another year."

For seventeen years I've waited like a soldier's wife for something.
I guess it'll take some time to get reacquainted.

For seventeen years I've said "I won't live another year."
I experienced the actual breaking down, mud and twigs underfoot.

I guess it'll take some time to get reacquainted.
At least when I was dying, I knew where I was going.
I experienced the actual breaking down, mud and twigs underfoot.
Almost out of ash, my body reconfigures itself.

At least when I was dying, I knew where I was going:
Into atheistic air and dirt, into the Atlantic Ocean . . .
Almost out of ash, my body reconfigures itself.
As if a reclining nude, I stare dumbfounded at my flesh.

Into atheistic dirt and air, into the Atlantic Ocean . . .
Peace became associated with that essential vanishing point.
As if a reclining nude, I stare dumbfounded at my flesh.
Now to associate peace with something else, such as myself, for
    instance.

Peace became associated with that essential vanishing point.
Peace used to mean simply a sheet of paper and a pencil.
Now to associate peace with something else, such as myself, for
    instance;
Myself as once I came to know myself, both future tense and past.

Peace used to mean simply a sheet of paper and a pencil.
With resistance I read back over my old poems:
Myself as once I came to know myself, both future tense and past,
Broken dreams hovering like the shadow of a branch—

Luna

The moon as brittle as a tooth
The moon mistaken
For a fortune coming true

Collapses tersely like a compact mirror
Its likeness sending me into a tailspin
My finger swelling
From the uncertainty nearly contained

And yet I admit her sympathy
I permit the telling
Of her story in the streets
Her story splintering apart in midstream
As she lies awake, the object of comment
A settlement of white wood and glass

Then where is she in our union?
Where is she
When the Black Lotus sways?

Amidst hibiscus and a broth of castile
A woman is lifted by her hips
Her hair pulled tightly from her temples
The way thread is jolted from a spool

With the back of my hand high
To her throat, she recoils
Like a loitering book to her binding
The crane returning

To her alcove of shade
Where wedged between the blueprints of ink
The indolent moon is a truant seed
Refusing to die and refusing to grow
No larger
Than a button or a dime

But hush
Now she listens from her circular booth
Solely to you or solely to me
Guileless as a pearl
With her sad, curved ear
Bowed like the forehead of a geisha girl.

Daniel Diamond

Anemones

Bob had an artist's eye
(or an artiste's as he would have joked),
and if his eye wasn't satisfied,
neither was he.

He never did one thing at a time,
scuttled between projects,
five minutes here or there,
and then suddenly he'd have,
conjurations!, several finished
works of art.

Once, as we made love,
Bob said, glancing at the vase
on the bedstand, "Oh! I know just
what to do with those anemones now!"

He jumped up, shuffled
the bright petal-wheels
on the corkscrew stems
until
      (I couldn't say just
               what he did)
the cluster took on
visual dimension,

sculptural completeness,
drama.

Bob rejoined me in our bed:
play-toss, bite-kiss, caress-slap,
lovemaking inflamed
by shared creation.

This probably sounds fey or highbrow,
but it was only lust.

His Face in Every Crowd

I see it when something happens
to individuals they can't fully
comprehend.

I saw it at Bloomingdale's
on the face of a woman
who was caught shoplifting
and tried to talk her way
out of it.

I saw it on the face
of a stray dog, its tags jingling
as it searched up and down
the same block,
looking for home.

I saw it on the face
of a defendant I,
along with 11 other jurors,
found not guilty
of a very serious crime.

I saw it in the grimace of terror
on the face of a young man
who was falsely arrested,
the nightstick falling repeatedly
against his calves.

The same shocked terror
I'd sometimes catch
(only from the corner of my eye
when he thought I wasn't looking)
on Bob's face.

The look our friends
withdrew from one by one.
That stupefaction!

His own body
giving way
to dissolution
with him caught
inside.

Recognizing Sadistic Tendencies

for Ian Young

It was one of those really butch
places down by Eleventh Avenue.
There was a sign on the wall reading:
      "This is a man's bar.
                     Dress like a man.
                     Act like a man."
This guy was circling around me slowly
again and again wearing this leather outfit
circling as if he were an eagle which had
spotted some prey far below.
There was a sign taped to the mirror behind
the bar which showed a woman being crushed
in the jaws of a doberman pinscher
and had a caption reading:
                     "Pussy Anyone?"
This guy had stopped walking and was looking
at me with a cold half smile, all blond
and Aryan, as if he thought he were some
golden boy of the SS. Finally he stopped
in front of me, his drink glowing blue
in the black light, and asked my name.
I told him. He said:
      "If there's two things
      I love in this world
      it's my dog and the name Daniel."
Yes, sir, it was a real man's bar.

William Dickey

Face-Paintings of the Caduveo Indians

The face-paintings of the Caduveo, says Levi-Strauss,
reflect a society they have forgotten:
like heraldry, he says, like playing cards.

It is like that. Even my mother, now,
turning the pages of the photograph album,
forgets the older faces. She insists she remembers,
but what she remembers is a style of face,
a way she can remember people looking.

I saw you at the Greek Orthodox church on Sunday.
You had lost weight. I was drinking sweetened coffee.
We were no longer a society.
I saw you as a stranger might, with interest.
You had drawn back behind the surface of your face.

In the last days, having nothing in common, we played cards,
and the cards became their own society,
playing themselves, not responsible to the players.
Your face was new, as if it had not been used.

I do not know what became of the Caduveo.
The face-paintings are in a museum, with the relics
of other societies that forgot themselves,
that became too few to be able to remember.

It is like that: a lessening of chances,
the thought that I will never again be in love
but will sit foolishly waiting for what is in the cards
while your face becomes a photograph, becomes
only a way I remember people looking.

The Food of Love

I could never sing. In the grade-school operetta
I sat dark offstage and clattered coconut shells.
I was the cavalry coming, unmusical, lonely.

For five years I played the piano and metronome.
I read *Deerslayer* in small print while I waited for my lesson,
and threw up after the recital at the Leopold Hotel.

I went to a liberal college, but I never learned
how to sit on the floor or help the sweet folk song forward.
My partridge had lice, and its pear-tree had cut-worm blight.

Yet this song is for you. In your childhood a clear falsetto,
now you sing along in the bars, naming old songs for me.
Even drunk, you chirrup; birds branch in your every voice.

It's for you, what I never sing. So I hope if ever
you reach, in the night, for a music that is not there
because you need food, or philosophy, or bail,

you'll remember to hear the noise that a man might make
if he were an amateur, clattering coconut shells,
if he were the cavalry, tone-deaf but on its way.

On His Way Home to Wyoming

We were too brief to expect to keep in touch.
The traffic stream has carried you past my stop.
I am no time you should remember much:
the moment of tenderness your mind lets drop
the way a cigarette falls from the hand
of a lover who is drunk or half asleep
and harmlessly burns out. I understand
the pleasure of having what we need not keep.

And when you leave, I understand the pleasure
of silence, of having my body to myself,
of washing your glass and putting it on a shelf,
of measuring out the day to my own measure,
at ease, not glad, not sorry that you have gone,
the bed stripped bare, the clean sheets not yet on.

Therefore

Nothing exists that is not marred; therefore
we are obliged to imagine how things might be:
the sea
at its green uttermost, the shore
white to exaggeration, white before
it was checked and clouded by its spent debris.

Nothing exists that does not end, and so
to knowledge we must deliberately be untrue:
you
murmuring that you will not go, when you will go,
promising to do always what you cannot do:
hold the sun steady, and the sky new.

No one exists who can be loved the same
by day as by dark; it is that sleeping place,
lame,
we attempt to follow into, and cannot trace,
that makes us lie, saying we know his face
as if we knew even half of his true name.

What I Want

I want to be mentioned more. I want to be able
to be dramatic: a sculpture Renaissance mouth
fifteen feet high. I want all the pistol fingers.
I want to drive up in a Bentley as big as a boat.

I'd like somebody to see to this pretty quickly.

Melvin Dixon

Heartbeats

Work out. Ten laps.
Chin ups. Look good.

Steam room. Dress warm.
Call home. Fresh air.

Eat right. Rest well.
Sweetheart. Safe sex.

Sore throat. Long flu.
Hard nodes. Beware.

Test blood. Count cells.
Reds thin. Whites low.

Dress warm. Eat well.
Short breath. Fatigue.

Night sweats. Dry cough.
Loose stools. Weight loss.

Get mad. Fight back.
Call home. Rest well.

Don't cry. Take charge.
No sex. Eat right.

Call home. Talk slow.
Chin up. No air.

Arms wide. Nodes hard.
Cough dry. Hold on.

Mouth wide. Drink this.
Breathe in. Breathe out.

No air. Breathe in.
Breathe in. No air.

Black out. White rooms.
Head hot. Feet cold.

No work. Eat right.
CAT scan. Chin up.

Breathe in. Breathe out.
No air. No air.

Thin blood. Sore lungs.
Mouth dry. Mind gone.

Six months? Three weeks?
Can't eat. No air.

Today? Tonight?
It waits. For me.

Sweet heart. Don't stop.
Breathe in. Breathe out.

Hungry Travel

I.

Carolina mountains to Pee Dee town,
sharecropping, my father as a boy
led mules and siblings.
He plowed for fifty cents a week
until the day his house burned down.

"Everything lost in the flames,"
he tells my mother. "I don't know
how to give any more."
He takes her like the mule,
riding shotgun
back to Carolina cinders.

II.

She croons, "Beautiful dreamer
wake unto me," as his arms lock

to her hips. He calls her, "Freak,
you must be some kind of freak."
She reaches for him, holds nothing.

In my twenty-fifth year,
his eyes avoiding mine, his voice:
"You're still my son," as if the silent
years between us were reasons to forget.
But I remember the song. I know
by heart her broken breath sung solo.

III.

This poem for the three of us
pulling from one chain.

Our metallic cries eat away
the hearthstone.
Our empty, angry mouths
hunger for any words that cure.

IV.

Nights while he's asleep
my mother kisses him.
"He can't fight me then. And alone
I can make love to him, to me."
Her eyes fill with warning:
"You'll get used to it, like I did."

At twelve my scout uniform
stained with forest seeds, above me
the crooning of white oak,
the crooning of a boy:
"Just one more time. One more time."

Until now.

V.

One man and I
cautious as pilgrims
return together.

My father shoots up from the table,
away from my mother, quiet now, gray.
His forehead creases, eyes hammer,
turns back to the yams and greens
as if we violated their ground of
vegetables, children, dreams.

My words gather into knives
slicing the hunger: "I'm still your son."
As if the silent years between us
were reasons to forget, were reasons to forget.

Tim Dlugos

D.O.A.

"You knew who I was
when I walked in the door.
You thought that I was dead.
Well, I am dead. A man
can walk and talk and even
breathe and still be dead."
Edmond O'Brien is perspiring
and chewing up the scenery
in my favorite film noir,
D.O.A. I can't stop watching,
can't stop relating. When I walked down
Columbus to Endicott last night
to pick up Tor's new novel,
I felt the eyes of every
Puerto Rican teen, crackhead,
yuppie couple focus on my cane
and makeup. "You're dead,"
they seemed to say in chorus.
Somewhere in a dark bar
years ago, I picked up "luminous
poisoning." My eyes glowed
as I sipped my drink. After that,
there was no cure, no turning back.
I had to find out what was gnawing
at my gut. The hardest part's

not even the physical effects:
stumbling like a drunk (Edmond
O'Brien was one of Hollywood's
most active lushes) through
Forties sets, alternating sweats
and fevers, reptilian spots
on face and scalp. It's having
to say goodbye like the scene
where soundtrack violins go crazy
as O'Brien gives his last embrace
to his girlfriend-*cum*-Girl
Friday, Paula, played by Pamela
Britton. They're filmdom's least
likely lovers—the squat and jowly
alkie and the homely fundamentally
talentless actress who would hit
the height of her fame as the pillhead-
acting landlady on *My Favorite Martian*
fifteen years in the future. I don't have
fifteen years, and neither does Edmond
O'Brien. He has just enough time to tell
Paula how much he loves her, then
to drive off in a convertible
for the showdown with his killer.
I'd like to have a showdown, too, if I
could figure out which pistol-packing
brilliantined and ruthless villain
in a hound's-tooth overcoat took
my life. Lust, addiction, being
in the wrong place at the wrong
time? That's not the whole

story. Absolute fidelity
to the truth of what I felt, open
to the moment, and in every case
a kind of love: all of the above
brought me to this tottering
self-conscious state—pneumonia,
emaciation, grisly cancer,
no future, heart of gold,
passionate engagement with a great
B film, a glorious summer
afternoon in which to pick up
the ripest plum tomatoes of the year
and prosciutto for the feast I'll cook
tonight for the man I love,
phone calls from my friends
and a walk to the park, ignoring
stares, to clear my head. A day
like any, like no other. Not so bad
for the dead.

If I Were Bertolt Brecht

I'd take a bath, first of all;
then I'd throw away those drab and ratty
suits I'm always photographed wearing.
Buy some new threads; and while I'm at it,
get myself in shape at the nearest Holiday
Health Spa. Next I'd trim the fat
off my plays, getting rid of the didactic
boring passages that make me such a German
artist. I'd develop a modest sense of humor
and a sense of modesty, and treat the ladies
better—they're people, too. If I hated
California as much as I say, I'd leave and go
somewhere I liked better; but I love California,
so that would eliminate a lot of grief.
I'd shave the silly moustache, get a tan,
and turn my life into a sane and happy one,
all before I went out for my sauerkraut
and knockwurst, into the Weimar night.

Poem After Dinner

for Tim

some things never run out:
my poverty, for instance,
is never exhausted
sandwiches for dinner again

your blond hair, for instance,
even if we're both exhausted
soothes me when we go outside
you and the forsythias

I get so excited
I think I'll read the Susan Sontag article
in *Partisan Review*
I want to walk beside you in the drizzle

and say you can move in with me
tonight, right away, even though
this time they'll probably evict me
and although I'm moving out in three weeks anyway

Pretty Convincing

Talking to my friend Emily, whose drinking
patterns and extravagance of personal
feeling are a lot like mine, I'm pretty
convinced when she explains the things we do
while drinking (a cocktail to celebrate the new
account turns into a party that lasts till 3
a.m. and a terrific hangover) indicate
a problem of a sort I'd not considered.
I've been worried about how I metabolize
the sauce for four years, since my second bout
of hepatitis, when I kissed all the girls
at Christmas dinner and turned bright yellow
Christmas night, but never about whether
I could handle it. It's been more of a given,
the stage set for my life as an artistic queer,
as much of a tradition in these New York circles
as incense for Catholics or German
shepherds for the blind. We re-enact
the rituals, and our faces, like smoky icons
in a certain light, seem to learn nothing
but understand all. It comforts me
yet isn't all that pleasant, like drinking
Ripple to remember high school. A friend
of mine has been drinking in the same bar for decades,
talking to the same types, but progressively
fewer blonds. Joe LeSueur says he's glad
to have been a young man in the Fifties with his
Tab Hunter good looks, because that was the image
men desired; now it's the Puerto Rican

angel with great eyes and a fierce fidelity
that springs out of machismo, rather than a moral
choice. His argument is pretty convincing, too,
except lots of the pretty blonds I've known
default by dying young, leaving the field
to the swarthy. Cameron Burke, the dancer
and waiter at Magoo's, killed on his way home from
the Pines when a car hit his bike on Sunrise Highway.
Henry Post dead of AIDS, a man I thought would be around
forever, surprising me by his mortality the way
I was surprised when I heard he was not
the grandson of Emily Post at all, just pretending,
like the friend he wrote about in *Playgirl*, Blair Meehan,
was faking when he crashed every A List party for a year
by pretending to be Kay Meehan's son, a masquerade
that ended when a hostess told him "Your mother's here"
and led him by the hand to the dowager—Woman, behold
thy son—underneath a darkening conviction that all,
if not wrong, was not right. By now Henry may have faced
the same embarrassment at some cocktail party in the sky.
Stay outrageously nasty as you were. And Patrick
Mack, locked into my memory as he held court in the Anvil
by the downstairs pinball machine, and writhing
as he danced in Lita Hornick's parlor when the Stimulators
played her party, dead last week of causes I don't know,
as if the cause and not the effect were the problem.
My blond friend Chuck Shaw refers to the Bone-
crusher in the Sky, and I'm starting to
imagine a road to his castle lit by radiant
heads of blonds on poles as streetlamps for the gods,
flickering on at twilight as I used to do

in the years when I crashed more parties and acted
more outrageously and met more beauties and made
more enemies than ever before or ever again, I pray.
It's spring and there's another crop of kids
with haircuts from my childhood and inflated self-esteem
from my arrival in New York, who plug into the history
of prettiness, convincing to themselves and the devout.
We who are about to catch the eye of someone
new salute as the cotillion passes, led by blonds
and followed by the rest of us, a formal march
to the dark edge of the ballroom where we step out
onto the terrace and the buds on the forsythia
that hides the trash sprout magically
at our approach. I toast it
as memorial to dreams as fragile and persistent
as a blond in love. My clothes smell like the smoky
bar, but the sweetness of the April air's
delicious when I step outside and fill
my lungs, leaning my head back
in a first-class seat on the shuttle
between the rowdy celebration of great deeds
to come and an enormous Irish wake in which
the corpses change but the party goes on forever.

Sleep Like Spoons

There is a bed on 83rd
which like a Gileadic balm
can soothe the soul. I lay me down
to sleep there, and to find the calm

that lives within your shoulder blade,
beneath the cool and freckled skin
that makes my midnights white as those
in settings Scandinavian

where cry of loon and forest sighs
not car alarms and salsa beat
drift upward through the window cracks
and mitigate the summer heat.

No way to mute the blaring horns,
nor open hearts that don't discern
the trove of tenderness within
the tangled postures lovers learn

in sex and rest, limbs juxtaposed,
exhaustion mingled with delight.
We close our eyes and sleep like spoons
inside the silverchest of night.

Jim Everhard

Dayton: Non-Memories

for my mother

> *It is located in the southwestern part of the State, on both*
> *banks of the Great Miami R., where it receives the waters of*
> *Mad and Stillwater rivers and of Wolf Creek.*
> —from *Universal Standard Encyclopedia*

> *When Humanity advances, all mothers will be isolated before*
> *the birth of their children in some protected place where they*
> *shall be surrounded by statues, pictures, and music.*
> —ISADORA DUNCAN, *My Life*, 1927

1.

Born in Dayton, after Hitler,
I was surrounded by precision industry:
cash registers, computing scales,
electric-refrigeration equipment,
automobile parts, paper and
paper-making machinery, filling-
station equipment, lifting jacks,
boilers, fire-fighting equipment,

bicycles, golf clubs, paints
and ice cream cones.

Everyone in Dayton must have a skill.

My mother had no skill
except Catholicism,
and she wasn't even Cathollic,
just educated by nuns,
almost a nun herself
until she joined the WAVES.

2.

I have just taken a test that
shows I have no mechanical aptitude.
I took a test in the Navy that
detected effeminate inklings,
because I preferred the ballet
to football. Actually,
football can be quite graceful
in slow motion. Combat, too.
All wars of honor should be fought
in slow motion, each nuance of
fear pin-pointed for viewer absorption.
The ballet is everywhere,
our shadows lie at our feet
like the black tights we
are afraid to pull over our bodies.

3.

I don't remember Dayton.
I would like to remember
the Mad and Stillwater rivers.
No entry for Wolf Creek
in the Universal Standard Encyclopedia.
The Wright Brothers invented
flying in Dayton. What must it
feel like to parachute into water,
into water wrapped in wet silk,
not even hearing the explosion,
to fall into strange water
trying to remember its name?
I'd like to fly over Dayton
in memory of the Wright Brothers.

4.

Flying is graceful because
it is so hard to believe how fast
you are really going. Clouds
slow it all down.
Airplane parts are made in Dayton.
Someday Dayton may become that myth
like Troy or Atlantis.
I'd like to be a part of that myth.
There's a hospital for mental cases
in Dayton. Maybe a man is there,
shell-shocked from some past war,

who still thinks flying is impossible.
I would like to talk to him.
I would like to bring him
the wax and feathers
he calls for in the night.
If he is afraid of the Mad River,
I will show him the Stillwater.
He might think I'm his mother.
That would be all right, too.

5.

When I was pulled from my mother's womb
I vaguely recall a doctor humming,
or maybe it was a nurse
with a tray full of metal objects.
I remember the wings pulled from my back,
discarded with the placenta.
To make me human, perfect.
I was a perfect baby.

6.

When I got my first ten-dollar bill
(for my tenth birthday)
I wanted to buy my mother
everything she missed as a child
during the depression. I wanted to
fly into Dayton and buy her
cash registers, gas pumps,

boilers, bicycles, golf clubs
and ice cream cones.
Instead I gave her
One Hundred and One Favorite Poems.
I liked the way books open, slow, perfect wings.

The Mystical Life

There comes a day when all of us
disappear as completely as
the mystic with his rope trick.
Some of us climb old sheets.
Some climb the wind. No matter
how we get there, we all end up
in the same place. We are more
rootless than life seems, except
in the All. Even the tiny fly
carries part of us into the sky.
We rub off on the rose bush.
We drape across the grass.
We cross that bridge before we
get to it. You may think you know
where you're going, at least which
alternatives you have, but you don't.
When you die you will lose your will.
Being a mystic means accepting
what it is like to be dead

before you are dead, but with your will.
Embrace the mystical life.
Pray for the ability to no longer ask
for anything. Volunteer poverty.
Eat soup from a pot that stays
on a fire of eternal flames,
a soup poor in substance
yet rich and warm.

December 22, 1978

Sexual Liberation in a Desperate Age

for Orry

eyes ogle ceaselessly
even my own
like when i'm reading this poem
only instead of the words
i'm reading a conversation
on lips across the room.
even in a dangerous time
i'm still interested, still amused
by all the ways we fail to meet
then out of the blue
maybe it's in my zodiac
i'm hardly cruising at all and
i feel these lips all over my body
only nobody is touching me
it's those ceaselessly ogling eyes
across the bar or on the street
and i begin to lecture myself about
no sex and safe sex and definitely
off limit sex
even before the subject comes up
or we've even exchanged names.
ogling eyes prickle the flesh
on the back of my neck,
fortunately under my raised collar.
it still, it never paid, pays
to be easy
and i've been easy in my time

like sticking a fork in a piece of
lemon meringue pie
and pulling it up,
how everything sticks to the fork.
under bridges, in cars, behind alleys,
i've toured all the classical places,
blessed them with a little low-style relief.
all because of ogling eyes.
i've held up the corner of a bar
grinding my ass into the wall
being ground up in those ridiculous
strangleholds we all adore,
the kind that leave red fingerprints
and dark tooth marks on your neck
but somehow never come close to the real thing.
in my younger days we called this free love
and beer was cheaper then but
it didn't take long to figure out
nothing's for free.
today you might as well shadow box with death
or play chess with the devil
or pretend you're starring
in one of ingmar bergman's bleaker films,
walked barefoot over the chipped glass
of yesterday's myths. i never thought
we'd have to slow down.
i thought we were winning.
and then i remembered how many times
i ended up letting some guy fuck me
when all i really wanted
was to be held.

your eyes ogled at me
the way we used to do it.
i ogled back
as best i could remember.
how can we begin to love
when we don't even know where we're starting,
what we're bringing with us.
it's not the same anymore.
one of us has already said
what if we'd met four years ago
but that's the kind of question
you can't help asking any more
because four years ago and today
are different worlds
and we are different men
trying not to act desperately
in a desperate age.
if love isn't safe
why should sex be safe.
what you may be restoring
it took three hundred men to break down.
a part of me
is still alive and safe to touch
as many ways as you please.
my heart regenerates
even when my body is busy dying,
unfooled as it is by a few boyish gestures.
what we know won't hurt us
nor will the ignorance of the past be erased.
we are new men.
we don't have to live desperate lives.

but we have to find each other
if we want to quell the fear
and we have to stop, perhaps,
at the very spot where we once began everything.
liberation begins again
always where liberation died once.
fear has returned.
we meet each other in the chains of freedom.

May 29, 1984

Don Garner

High Park Buddies

A football on the table
two cokes between them

Matching sets of silver hair
the table full of chessboard

Me and this poem until
my shadow fills the page

May 31, 1980

I Confess No Confession

I confess to the hornets' nest
of police whistles.
I confess to the stab of light.

I confess to the cloak
of dark blue shadows—
my workshirt and jeans.

I confess to the stab of light
that missed me.

I confess to the corner
that saved me.
I confess to the point
of orgasm lost
when cops swarmed in.

I confess to the ritual
of sex in the parks.
I confess no confession
need save me.

October Fires

The brace of geese against
the northward flight of clouds—
the wedge works its way through
hearty blocks of winter wood
feeding grey October fires.

Chasen Gaver

As Goes Diana Ross, So Goes the Nation

you jump up
you jump up
you jump up
you
come
down

And the whole country traced her dipped hip trip
    from Motown to Holly-Hollywood
    from the Brewster Projects' death knell
        to the Beverly Hills Hotel-tel

I DON'T CARE IF MARY WILSON JUST CUT A NEW ALBUM!
As goes Diana Ross, so goes the nation.

So as most things get worse
Some say, to break the curse,
We should extricate ourselves
    from the American highlands
Expatriate ourselves
    to the Caribbean islands

you jump up
you jump up
you jump up

you
come
down

But I still keep hangin' around/round/round
listening & listening
    for a lyrical miracle
        tug at my sleeve
And I won't go
    until I know
Diana herself is preparing to leave.

Keep your dial on that bop-a-dop station
As goes Diana Ross, so goes the nation.

you jump up
you jump up
you jump up
you
come
down

Giving us cause to separate
    from hometown and from husband
As goes Diana Ross, so goes the nation.

fading beauty

she pouts.
I know all about
pouting.
In certain
former French colonies
pouting has a regal quality,
but hers
is little more
than a taste for life
gone sour.

she is short with people
on the phone.
I suggest that she go back
to school, take up
hobbies: gardening, anything
to stop thinking
about the men who no longer
call each evening, having
scaled her crumbling castle walls.

she buys an attack dog
and pouts.

Richard George-Murray

[August hot, autumn pushing]

August hot, autumn pushing,
full moon again,
and I'm still living
in last spring—
weaker, the scent leaner,
the ice closer.

[Mother]

Mother
ran off with the ferryman
crossed that last river
drank the local water
forgot us all.

[On the side porch, the compact black cat]

On the side porch, the compact black cat
tail over toes, stares at the falling rain.
Upstairs, the neighbor's boy, about
seventeen, dark and sullen, elbows
on the pillowed sill, leans
out of his bedroom window, wearing
just a thin
trickle of smoke.

[Someone should]

Someone should
listen to the wind dying in the birches,
hear the crows and crickets,
eat the berries too ripe to carry,
hear the apples fall,
stand ready to testify
it all happened.

[White quiet]

White quiet
under January moon,
the pond spillway's falling water
makes an under ice sound,
and up in the barn a cow
resettles herself.
White, white, quiet,
and the stars' slow circling.

Jaime Gil de Biedma

Against Jaime Gil de Biedma

What good, I'd like to know, is it to move,
to leave behind a basement even murkier
than my reputation—which is saying a lot—
to hang white lace curtains,
hire a maid
and turn away from my bohemian days
only to have you, big galoot,
bungling boarder absurdly dolled up in my suits,
idle drone, idiotic and in the way,
to have you turn up with hands just washed
to take bites off my plate and mess up the place?

Hustlers and florists keep you company
on the stools of the last bars to close
and at dawn so do the empty streets
and the yellow elevator light
when you stumble home drunk
and stop to study the ravages
of your face in the mirror
with the still-crazed eyes
you refuse to shut. And if I say a word,
you laugh me off, remind me of the past
and say I'm just getting old.

I could remind you that you're not so charming anymore.
That your sporty style, your cool
turned cruel
after you hit thirty.
And that your winning smile
of a dreamy kid—
sure to please—is a labored leftover,
a pretty sad try.
Meanwhile you gaze at me with your trueblue
orphan's eyes and you cry on my shoulder
and promise me not to do it anymore.

If only you weren't such a little whore!
And if I didn't know, as I have for years,
that you take over when I give in
and you grow faint when I rage. . . .
The impression I get when you get home
is a jumble of panic, hurt and disgust,
of depression
and impatience and resentment
at coming back to endure, one more time,
the inexcusable shame
of being far too close to me.

I'll have a terrible time putting you to bed
and you're hell
to sleep with.
Swooning at every limp step
and stumbling against furniture
we'll grope our way through the apartment

in a clumsy embrace, staggering
from drink and choked-back sobs.
O what lowdown drudgery to love another
and the lowest
is to love yourself!

Anniversary Song

Because six years have gone by since then,
because there's still nothing on earth,
nothing so sweet as a room
for two, if it's yours and mine;
because even time, that poor relation
who has seen better days,
is waving a flag for happiness today:
let's sing for joy!

And then let's get up late
like on Sunday. Let's linger
the whole morning long making love
again but better: in another way
night can't even imagine
while our room, just like time,
fills with sunlight, quiet intimacy
and the serenity of the ages.

Echo of our pleasure days,
desire, music remembered

inside the heart, so romantic
I've barely put it in my poems;
all the fragrance, unfaithful past,
what was sweet and inspires longing,
don't you see how everything you and I
once dreamed is overwhelmed by what is?

Reality—not a pretty sight—
with its awkward details of being two,
shameful nights of love without desire
and desire without love
we couldn't atone for in six centuries
of sleeping alone. And its enigmatic
shifts from betrayal to boredom,
boredom back to betrayal.

No, life's not a dream, and you know
we both tend to forget it.
But a little dreaming, that's all,
a smidgen for this occasion, hushing up
about the rest of the story, and a moment
when you and I wish each other
a long and happy life together—
I doubt it can do any harm.

Pandemic and Celeste

quam magnus numerus Libyssae arenaew

. . .

aut quam sidera multa, cum tacet nox,
furtiuos hominum uident amores

—CATULLUS, VII

Now just imagine very late at night
you and I are talking
man-to-man at last.
Picture it
on one of those unforgettable nights
of rare communion, with the bottle
half empty, ashtrays overflowing
and the subject of life more than worn out.
What I'm going to show you is a heart,
an unfaithful one
naked from the waist down,
hypocrite reader—*mon semblable—mon frère!*

Because it's not the haste of someone cruising
for orgasms that flings me from my own body
toward other bodies, young if at all possible:
I also stalk sweet love,
the tender kind to sleep at my side
and make my bed a joy to wake up in
like a bird nearby.
No, I never can take off my clothes,
never can enter another's arms

without feeling—if just for a moment—
as dazzled as I did at twenty!

To know love, to learn about it,
it's necessary to have been alone.
And it's necessary to have made love
on four hundred nights—with four hundred
different bodies. Its mysteries,
as the poet said, are of the soul
but a body is the book in which they are read.

And that's why I'm happy to have rolled around
on the coarse sand, both of us half-dressed,
while I felt for that brawn in the shoulder.
I'm moved remembering so many instances. . . .
That mountain road and the carefully managed
hidden gropings and the vulnerable moment,
after slamming on the brakes, standing
glued to the embankment, blinded by light.
Or that late afternoon by the river,
naked, laughing and crowned with ivy.
Or that doorway in Rome—on Via de Babuino.
And memories of faces and cities
barely known, bodies only glimpsed,
of unlit stairwells, ship cabins,
of bars, deserted passageways, whorehouses
and endless seaside changing booths,
of castle moats.
Especially memories of all of you,
O nights in one-night cheap hotels,

definitive nights in seedy rented rooms,
in rooms just vacated,
nights that give back to your guests
the forgotten smell of themselves.
Like a broken image, the story in body and soul
de la langueur goutée à ce mal d'être deux.
Without putting down—
festive as a weekday holiday—
the pleasures of sleeping around.

Although I suspect my love's labors scattered
wouldn't be worth much
if it weren't for real love.
My love,
          whole image of my life,
sun of the same nights I steal.

His youth, mine—
music from the core of me—
still smiles in the fumbling grace
of each young body,
of each anonymous encounter,
illuminating it. Giving it soul.
And there are no beautiful thighs
that don't recall his beautiful thighs
when we first met, before going to bed.

Not even the passion of a one-night stand
can compare with the passion
that comes from the understanding,

the years of experience
of our love.
                    For with love
time is also important and
in some ways it's rather sweet
to trace with a melancholy hand
its perceptible path across the body—
while a familiar expression on the lips
or a limb's slight pulsing
is enough to make me marvel
at that classic grace
fleeting as a reflection.

After more years slide by, when we reach the end,
I want to press my lips
against his bleary skin
calling up the image of his body
and of all those bodies blotted out by time
that I loved just once, if only for a moment.
To ask for the courage to go on living
without beauty, without strength or desire
while we remain together
until both of us die in peace,
as it's said those die who have loved so much.

Yesterday Morning, Today

You rest your temple against
   the open window pane
watching rain falling down
   over the ocean.

In a split-second image—
   your body outlined
serenely in half-light, still
   naked from the night.

And then you turn toward me,
   smiling. I'm thinking
so much has changed but this
   is how I remember you.

Translations by James Nolan

Roy Gonsalves

The House of the Dead

No hieroglyphics
But there were signs
Purple lesions.

There were no pyramids
No funeral processions
Spirits came to visit.

This was not the Fifth Dynasty
Osiris was not adored
No hymns sung.

On the wall
Were ascriptions of the eternal life
"Seal me in this house
Burn incense
Light candles
I will live again"
Smeared in blood and feces.

Wanting

I gave myself to you
Underneath the oak tree
Thereafter, I craved you
Like a bum does wine
But tonight I saw Jesus
It is he who takes me now
I want Jesus
Like a dying bird
Craves the sky.

Craig G. Harris

Alive After His Passion

for Elias

green mangos
with salt and
vinegar
hearts of palm
and holy ghosts
make me
speak in
tongues
with garlic breath,
dance to unheard
beats
fall beneath your
holy temple
inhaling gray
incense dust,
writhing in
shed snake skins
purified in the
flame,
wrapped
in unspeakable
joy

The Hardening of Soft Men

for Richard Bruce Nugent

Lily hits streets
in purple pumps
with sturdy shaved
legs revealed
in sheer stockings
selling whatever
boys buy
on sweaty nights
when no one's
watching

            Jade graces stages
            in glittered gowns
            mouths melodies
            to dance steps
            rehearsed before
            broken mirrors
            for singles shoved
            between brassiere
            cups and
            deception

stiletto tongue
staccato curses
spit in
Spanish at
strangers who
signal the
lump at her

throat,
the stubble
at her cheeks

        drunken appreciation
        drawled blessings
        descend on audiences
        who applaud
        the dramatic flare
        of her performance
        the identical
        appearance and mannerisms
        of the reigning
        disco diva

Lily counts tens
from jobs blown
under steering wheels,
public trees,
half moons
that turn to
sunrise before
the close of
business and
midday rest

        Jade counts bars,
        measures
        hit singles,
        scratched
        twelve inches,
        checks
        lip synch,
        lip stick,

minutes to
showtime.

her bestowal of
gratuities selfless
undaunted by fear
of violence or arrest
she does not
seek affection
on steamy streetcorners
it is the hardening
of soft men
she desires

her performance
delivered with pride
her message filled
with encouragement
she does not
seek acceptance
on smoky stages
it is the hardening
of soft men
she desires

Our Dead Are Not Buried Beneath Us

for Marc-Steven Dear, 1953-1986

he was older than he'd said
thinner than goodbye
slipping through airport tears
his left eye,
rebellious,
refused to yield to
weight of copper coin

his cold hands
calmly folded
accepted Laura's crystals,
Geneva's daisies
my last letter
Big Laura's last grasp

I noticed the tribal markings
of his face
multiplied
grown larger than when I'd last seen
constant reminders of
dimly lit liaisons

the lid closed
on so much unfinished business
in the appropriate absence
of a father who might

have loved a son too dark,
too precious
and the presence
of a man who tried.

Essex Hemphill

American Wedding

In america,
I place my ring
on your cock
where it belongs.
No horsemen
bearing terror,
no soldiers of doom
will swoop in
and sweep us apart.
They're too busy
looting the land
to watch us.
They don't know
we need each other
critically.
They expect us to call in sick
watch television all night,
die by our own hands.
They don't know
we are becoming powerful.
Every time we kiss
we confirm the new world coming.

What the rose whispers
before blooming

I vow to you.
I give you my heart,
a safe house.
I give you promises other than
milk, honey, liberty.
I assume you will always
be a free man with a dream.
In america,
place your ring
on my cock
where it belongs.
Long may we live
to free this dream.

Black Beans

Times are lean,
Pretty Baby,
the beans are burnt
to the bottom
of the battered pot.
Let's make fierce love
on the overstuffed
hand-me-down sofa.
We can burn it up, too.
Our hungers
will evaporate like—money.

I smell your lust,
not the pot burnt black
with tonight's meager meal.
So we can't buy flowers for our table.
Our kisses are petals,
our tongues caress the bloom.
Who dares to tell us
we are poor and powerless?
We keep treasure
any king would count as dear.
Come on, Pretty Baby.
Our souls can't be crushed
like cats crossing streets too soon.
Let the beans burn all night long.
Our chipped water glasses are filled
with wine from our loving.
And the burnt black beans—
caviar.

Family Jewels

for Washington D.C.

I live in a town
where pretense and bone structure
prevail as credentials
of status and beauty—
a town bewitched
by mirrors, horoscopes
and corruption.

I intrude on this nightmare,
arm outstretched from curbside.
I'm not pointing to Zimbabwe.
I want a cab to take me to Southeast
so I can visit my mother.
I'm not ashamed to cross
the bridge that takes me there.

No matter where I live
or what I wear
the cabs speed by.
Or they suddenly brake
a few feet away
spewing fumes in my face
to serve a fair-skinned fare.

I live in a town
where everyone is afraid
of the dark.

I stand my ground unarmed
facing a mounting disrespect,
a diminishing patience,
a need for defense.

In passing headlights
I appear to be a criminal
I'm a weird-looking
muthafucka.
Shaggy green hair sprouts all over me.
My shoulders hunch and bulge. I growl
as blood drips from my glinting fangs.

My mother's flowers are wilting
while I wait.
Our dinner
is cold by now.

I live in a town
where pretense and structure
are devices of cruelty—
a town bewitched
by mirrors, horoscopes,
and blood.

For My Own Protection

I want to start
an organization
to save my life.
If whales, snails,
dogs, cats,
Chrysler, and Nixon
can be saved,
the lives of Black men
are priceless
and can be saved.
We should be able
to save each other.
I don't want to wait
for the Heritage Foundation
to release a study
stating Black men
are almost extinct.
I don't want to be
the living dead
pacified with drugs
and sex.

If a human chain
can be formed
around missile sites,
then surely Black men
can form human chains
around Anacostia, Harlem,

South Africa, Wall Street,
Hollywood, each other.

If we have to take tomorrow
with our blood are we ready?
Do our S curls,
dreadlocks, and Phillies
make us any more ready
than a bush or conkaline?
I'm not concerned
about the attire of a soldier.
All I want to know
for my own protection
is are we capable
of whatever,
whenever?

Where Seed Falls

Stalking.
The neighborhood is dangerous
but we go there.
We walk the long way.
Our jangling keys
mute the sound of our stalking.
To be under the sky, above

or below a man.
This is our heat.
Radiant in the night.
Our hands blister with semen.
A field of flowers blossoms
where we gather
in empty warehouses.
Our seed falls
without the sound or
grace of stars.
We lurk in shadows.
In the dark
we don't have to say
I love you.
The dark swallows it
and sighs like we sigh,
when we rise
from our knees.

Leland Hickman

Blackwillow Daybreak

for Steven Anter

unguided ungratified unillumined unslept
untoucht stunted passions debaucht brutish down to daybreak
anywhere anyone   quick men   dead men   my nameless
city park dirt path spring lust fog
agitating largo out of Ferndell/ how I
          grasp myself priest in grum hickmaning dawn
self-addicted grave groyne sweat, this
habit fatidic withal, mine ascetic my listless slug;
mine inburied ephemeral upanishad moon,
extiniguisht, inflames it, delights it; how ungrowing I gasp
uphill toward blackwillow, hidden, shadowd
reborn fresh morning spring creekside bird-
sung proud paleblossomd owl-home wingd-ant-home snake-home,
          song-home my kiss-the-ground sanctum blackwillow;
reach hilltop, stop,
breathe in in sharp hurt in clear sudden sight of it, crisp
piercing first light thru tentative fog lift,
early leaf cry, soft seed shimmer, moving, breathing, swaying
unto itself alone how no one shd deceive it,
shaking, yet no breeze to disturb it;
          & I wonder, & I see:
giant, muscled, hardond, strippt
lunatic, writhing against treetrunk,

fragile seeds adrift in strange griefs around him,
fingertips on nipples, eyes half-closed, groaning,
watching my approach, not shifting his gaze away,
         dionysian long dark hair bejewelled yellowgreen,
young blackwillow leaves ensnard there, yellow blackwillow
         flowers fallen;
then in seedstorm under branches
shivering in my willowshell, spell-
bound, stunnd, how
wordless he sings to me, beckons to me, slave to his story, fierce
half-smile, shoulders, chest,
loins sweating pollenkisst/ his white torso,
harsh-breatht, archt against willow, his
thick thighs spread wide & between them:
slender, living, stiff, low blackwillowlimb plungd-in upgouging,
         greast, abandond-to, ridden,
slid savaging grinding, crazd mean tight on,
thrashes his body back against dread, angrier, wilder,
& by his uprooted, panickt, uneartht outcry
         begets this song,
anointed under showers of willowseed shaken downtrembling
         upon us.

on wet soil kneeling in my willowshell, near
broken giant breaking my husht seeds free, soon
to cease drifting over me   lost, ghost-human, kisses
earthkissing rhythm-tree, dresses, vanishes, fades from my story;
& my blackwillow song grown calm, solemn,
small birds, jays, bright blues, return,
my red ants up treetrunk, silver-wingd, flashing,
         how they signal my sunup;

sunbeams thru leaf-whispers onto low willowstub, glisten
of mucous, blood, sheer wings glint,
flying ants stumbling up phallus-shaft, over
round-ridgd corona's blind eye, how
craftily he carvd it, despairing, exultant, defiant,
            insane in his half-light;
now, blackwillow, blackwillow, hide me,
for I unbuckle memory; for I undo my name;
for I strip me to childhood;
            for I slide down onto you,
fingertips on nipples, my thighs spread wide,
for you pierce me, ravage me, for you make me cry loud;
for I beat my body back against dread; for these poor songs'
            pounding;
for shook blossoms scatterd meaningless from yr sky;
for I sob, for I gibber, for I babble crude psalm;
            for I desecrate;
for I sing ashamed of my daylight.

Yellowknife Bay

for Dennis Ellman

under clouded noonsky, crossgraind, dry thunders muffled,
    whimper
of wind, last hours, Fort Providence, & hours-late bus, we wait
by hudson bay company, wooden porch steps, Slave
Indian children star, frown, sullen-eyed; we board
mudcaked outback rattletrap, curses spat, dirtclods, rocks
flung after us; backfiring toward Yellowknife, Aussie
driver, Indian woman, two young Slave Indian men, Hank, me;
downpour again & overcast always; night; each riding silent,
    alone, & wind
whistling thru windowcracks; graveld highway, pitted;
swerve, slide, wheelslip; cold; impossible sleep;
lightning-lit poverties of villages, ancient tribes in their modern
               squalor; word-road, pitchdark;
wilderness unanswering; no signs for me; my forest un-
               yielding; word-rain, plainsong, pitchdark.

next day, Yellowknife New Town, mercenary, safe;
& bayward thru Old Town, quaint, & Latham Island bridge,
    Hank
leading; toward smoldering windborne garbage-stench, steep
downhill road where Dogbills die, warriors once,
slaveowners once, in their weatherd-dun box-huts by the dump;
last summer, drove ridge-route, L.A. to childhood, East
Bakersfield 2534 Lake Street not one bleakness changed, blight
amid blight; Indians; other poor; crossgraind oilsmoke sky; trees
dead; new boxes without frontyards, built on old frontyards,

memoried childscape crumbling behind them; no sidewalks,
    nothing green; transfixed, pitchdark,
gazing; frontstoop roof, 2-x-4 proppt, on dad's mean shack,
    decrepit; look, look, outhouse prison of pitchdark,
still standing; & I'm afraid, & my mother's afraid; fears
to be seen outdoors torn blue bathrobe flapping; suddenly
crying; why; why is she crying; in rain I see her, dark-haird,
wearing a blue bathrobe, standing still on planks that cover mud,
the way to the outhouse, in the storm, holding her
hands to her face, screaming, screaming; or I'm home from my
    canal, barefoot,
she's dressed-up, spitcurls auburn on her forehead, stands
on Lake Street with her suitcase; where are you going mommy;
o, sonny, she says, o, sonny, why did you come home so soon,
wait in the house, wait for yr father, & I stare thru the window,
             taximan, taximan, sky getting pitchdark;
race down driveway, holler, taxi turns corner, holler, standing
             rigid on Lake Street hollering in pitchdark;
now, Dogbills hammer-up stormwindows; under us,
volcanic outcroppings, glacier-groovd, Hank & I
stumble wind-deafend down boulders to Yellowknife Bay,
indigo pitchdark vast waterscape tempestuous in windsquall,
          ice-stifled under snowfall soon;
breathstopping wingbeat terror-squawk raven-clash vicious
    above us,
            beak-stab, blood-spray, feather-fall;
bleak plainsong sky over Great Slave Lake; unutterable omens
        singing me home.

James S Holmes

End of Autumn

You are like remembrance of a wine
after the dinner's finished, haunting the mouth;
or the last wail of an Attic chorus, mild,

kathartic, after the hero's dead, and the sound
and fury have faded away. You are the ending
resolved chord of the piece in the ancient style,

polite, minor. Yours no passionate finish,
but an ashamed exit only death
can equal: there is no after in you.

Gauleiter (*from* "Two Wind Poems")

The wind lays into the leaves
broadfisted:
his power's been tested
and he foresees
he shall have claim to days
long after
all leaves are buried:
hear then his laughter,
iron, unhurried,
over their lime-white graves.

Hymn to a War God
to be chanted in unison

Unpatterned and
pagan god,
you are our love.

The other ones
(Jesu, Buddha)
are perfectly cast:
images for
a polished hour.

You are for time
when images fail.
You are our love.

Recollection

for Michael Valeton

The gray rain swings out over the nightlit city
like a gendarme's cape in the wind. There is
no flick-flick-flick of the swallow, nor even the sparrow noises:
only the caged birds flourish tonight in Paris.

Up from the Metro, subterranean serpent,
I remember the schoolboys marking places
in textbooks before their stations, smiling shrewdly like lovers.
How differently cool and light and Northern your face is.

Arturo Islas

Algol/Algolagnia

What dark satellite afflicts your brightness?
Algol! fixed and writhing in her perfect hair
(Like agapanthus, blue Medusa in the wind),
Perseus' sword, mirrored in the constellations.
                                        Among the sisters,
She alone was mortal, despite the hair.
Bodiless, the gorgon floats among the stars,
You, among the snakes, shining, your beauty
Diminished by lust and pain
                                        The Hero,
Long gone, concerned with maidens in distress
And building cities, did not stop to save you.
Light years away, you do not see him
Holding you away from him, shielding himself,
Using her to turn others into stone.

A perpetual memory, the shadow
Of his flailing weapon on its way
To the veins in her neck, passes over you
(A father's sins visited upon a son),
The blameless child cursed in its gleaming.

Moonshine

Tonight I, lunatic in a scotch haze,
Stood at the kitchen sink
   where in February, at this time of day,
   you peeled avocados for our salad;
   where in June, a few steps away,
   we said goodbye to three years of illusion
   and deception (I cried unknowing then)
Looked out of the window and saw it—
   young, white, full and wide.

"Friend, come look at the moon,"
I said, out loud, and then,
   without sadness and matter-of-factly
   as it had risen in the East,
Remembered you were not here.

I am the moon now.
In the windows, cold and indifferent,
I gaze at myself and the people.

They're usually drunk.

Video Songs

"Isabel" to be sung by Mick Jagger

He ties you up in the basement
And says he'll be right back.
He tells you that he loves you
While you're still on the rack.

                             Masochist! Masochist!

Upstairs you know he's got someone
You hear them playing their games.
You lie there and wonder,
Where is Henry James?

                             Masochist! Masochist!

Get up, get up, dear Isabel,
Those silken chains are not real.
Your Daddy's only human,
Your waiting is his meal.

                             Masochist! Masochist!

"Emma" to be sung by David Bowie

Emma, you're a caution.
Dissatisfied to the end.
Your itch for the impossible
Whirled you round the bend.

Spend money on those clothes, girl,
Ignore your homely child.
The men will have their way with you,
They didn't drive you wild.

Choking on your poison,
You see them by your bed.
Their innocent stupidity
Mocks your pretty head.

You are a caution, Emma,
Your hair tied in a bun.
What a combination!
A romantic and a nun.

"Anna" to be sung by Annie Lennox

Tell them to go to hell, Anna
And take your man away.
Get rid of that husband
And rescue your Sergé

Else no one's going to save you
From that railway station light.
Not Vronsky or his army
Or the gasping in the night.

Anna, Anna, Anna!

Your name alone strikes fear
In the parlors of the rich.
You didn't fit their requirements,
You couldn't be a bitch.

"Albertine" to be sung by Boy George

Did you imagine when falling off that horse
That he would crown you queen
Or were you scared and screaming
Neck first on the green?

He wove you into his fancies
Without asking your permission,
Aroused by your addictions,
Detesting your submission.

Ah! how you got even
By lying through your teeth,
By sleeping through his romance,
By staying underneath

Until the women woke you.
Their tongues so much like yours,
Their hands forever pressing
Kept offering their cures.

Albertine! Libertine!

Apart from him, you don't exist
You lure him with your death.
And there he lies still scribbling,
Still taking a last breath.

Adam Johnson

December 1989

The nascent winter turns
Each root into a nail,
And in the West there burns
A sun morbid and pale.

Now, from the city bars
We drift, into a cool
Gymnasium of stars—
The drunkard and the fool:

Into the night we go,
Finding our separate ways—
The darkness fraught with snow,
The leaves falling like days.

The Departure Lounge

"He's gone to the departure lounge," you said—
Meaning, of course, he had not long to live.
Your tone was serious. I smiled instead,
Struck by the metaphor you chose to give
The irreversible process of decline
In one you must have loved (in your own way),
And how a quirk of speech can redefine
The real sense of loss.
                              Now, every day,
The faces have grown thinner round the bar.
We lose each other and we have not met—
Our separation ever more bizarre,
Based as it is on mutual regret,
Ironic in its total unity.
Death and the fear of death, of sensual fraud,
Darken the private chambers of the city
That echoes, like a vast communal ward,
With a dry-throated rage.
                              Clenching our pills,
We leave our doctors, newly diagnosed,
Think only of the virus that it kills
And how much to confide—or are composed,
Armed with a clearer knowledge as we chance
A cool controlled reaction: I recall
Profound relief, a kind of arrogance.
I had not reckoned that the sky would fall.

March 1992

The Night Ferry

for Colin Hunter

Wherever we must home to (even via
    the port of Dover where the English
perfected the art of delay) it is worth noting
    that going back accounts for
less time at sea than does an outward voyage—
    or seemingly:
                perhaps
a sense of the inevitable—work,
    the post, the awful news—
merely restores to us the familiar topography
    of the place we keep our days in,
where even strangers talk in our own language—
    though rarely after dawn
in a public bar.
              (On the Warmoesstraat,
    in a quarter of the city
whose every portal is hospitable,
    we have discussed the universe
with gods who drink *jenever* with their breakfast.)
    Whether our peregrinations
are solitary or made with one we trust
    will keep us from being bored
between lunch and dinner, a last evening encroaches.
    And now, a mile or so
off shore, alone, still fairly drunk, I stand,
    look back across the stern
to where Zeebrugge is a slick of lights

anonymous among
the coded stars, and think of every face,
    awed by the same night,
whose mouth 'O's with the names of continents—
    Boredom and Loneliness.
Freedom in transit, then—at a given instant
    not to be anywhere?
But this unhomely vessel is no time machine—
    land, though not in sight,
lies dead ahead.
                    We'll turn our watches back,
        glad if we have been missed,
and go together down St. Martin's Lane.

The Playground Bell

Dead drunk by nine—this used to be enough.
In Manchester I went out every night;
Picked up and stayed wherever there was drink
With men whose names were last thing on my mind—
Including one who slung the Union Jack
Over his bedside lamp for atmosphere
On the Last Night of the Proms in eighty-two;
My first 'experience': even the white socks
I'd been advised to wear were a success—
One foot displayed, half-casually, to mark
My absolute virginity. The final touch:
My mother fixed a blow-wave in my hair.

Always indulgent towards her only son
(Lucky for me my parents got divorced),
She must have sensed I wasn't the same boy
Who'd walked for twenty miles or more a day
On gritstone tracks, over the backs of hills-
The Pennine wastes of Bleaklow, Kinder Scout.

The landscape of the city was more harsh:
Bleaker than any tract of mountain peat,
The bus ride down the Manchester Old Road.
In Sackville Street, between the Thomson's Arms
And the Rembrandt Hotel, a universe
Peopled by drunks and rent boys—one a punk,
Who used to leave his girlfriend at the bar
On business. After barely half an hour,
He'd stroll back in and stand them both a drink.

I quickly learned the language and the code—
Had 'sisters' who were kind men twice my age,
Who paid for beers and thought I was mature;
Confided, gave advice and lent me fares.
On Saturday nights we'd drive to Liverpool
Or Stoke-on-Trent, as if there were a difference
Between one seedy night-spot and another—
Though local accents used to turn me on,
And that rare prize—a genuine foreigner
On holiday—was worth the taxi ride
To some remote hotel. Leaving in secret,
Before breakfast, pocketing an address
(In Paris!) I would never write to, a poignant act.

One Christmas I saved up and went to Heaven—
The biggest dive in England, under Charing Cross—
A three-tiered circuit ranged by packs of men,
And boys who came to dance. I ended up
In a basement somewhere off the Chepstow Road,
And woke to the first snowfall of the year.
I came to London for a long weekend
And stayed: met someone famous who was kind,
And took a boring job in Portland Place.
I went, on summer nights, to Hampstead Heath,
Where pints of beer at Jack Straw's Castle gave
To sex under the tents of holly trees—
Shadows of hands that flowered through the dusk:
No names, no contracts, but each parting hug
Was less a token of civility
Than an act of love.

Later, in Amsterdam,
In crowded cellars on the Warmoesstraat,
The rules were different—a more serious art,
Practised in uniform. The smell of leather
An aphrodisiac keen as the scent of leaves;
And still, the magic of indifference.

It still goes on—wherever hands can find
Response of hands; hold, in the hollow silence,
A tangible warmth, the heartbeat in the dark
Where death has entered, ringing the playground bell.
It hurts the ear. It echoes through the woods.

I stare at death in a mirror behind the bar
And wonder when I sacrificed my blood,
And how I could not recognise the face
That smiled with the mouth, the eyes, of death—
In Manchester, London or Amsterdam.
I do not hate that face, only the bell.

Poem on St. Patrick's Day

Woke on St. Patrick's Day
From a dream of my own death
Wracked in an old man's body
Under a heavy sheet,
And caught my breath
And lifted off the quilt.

I looked and found you sleeping,
And could not find a name
For what turned in an instant
From waking fear—
Relief? No, not relief.
You are more to me than that.

Half Irish, you
Will celebrate this day
With shamrock in your coat,
Drink after work
And telephone abroad,
Your mother's eldest son.

I lose weight and our bed's
Less comfortable these days.
So, while I can get out,
I'll go down in the light
Of a new season,
To where you are dancing.

March–April 1993

Glenn Philip Kramer

The Pamphlet I Threw Out

ARE YOU GAY? SCARED? DEPRESSED?
TIRED OF BARS? DOCTORS? MEMORIAL SERVICES?
DO YOU COUNT THE MINUTES YOU MAY
HAVE LEFT TO LIVE?
ARE YOU LIVING IN A DREAM WORLD? A NIGHTMARE?

AESTHETIC SURREALISM IS FOR YOU

What is Aesthetic Surrealism? It sounds like a movement to turn gay men into melting clocks.

Aesthetic Surrealism is **not** a movement to turn gay men into melting clocks. Aesthetic Surrealism is a movement that recognizes that gay men have already become melting clocks. It is the only movement that considers the actual predicament we are in. When any hour we might awaken to a spot on our leg signaling the end, when any second our lungs may give out, what realistic sense of time can we possibly have? We constantly see time bending downward into the horizon. We watch as our friends' time on earth melts into nothingness. We wait to melt. We are melting clocks ticking out our own mortality. It is not merely time however. Our whole experience has become surrealistic in that it has taken on a nightmarish quality. When we make love shadows overwhelm us telling us our partner is murdering us. When we make love shadows overwhelm us telling us we are murdering our partner. Thus we masturbate more, alone, our hands covered with ants. We become Andalusian dogs sniffing our own asses in fear, slicing our own eyes to shut out the world around us. If this be our reality, let us embrace it. Let us not compound the fear by fearing it. Aesthetic Surrealism rejoices in our state as a scrap of bloodied cloth that a psychiatrist uses to cover one ear when he sees the patient who has nightmares about fornicating giraffes and weeping leopards. If we are windows covered in lips, let us be windows covered in lips.

You arrive at a meeting of Aesthetic Surrealism. As you step through the door you hear a blood-curdling scream. The room is filled with mannequins in torn underwear and men looking through microscopes. Suddenly you realize that the men are wearing torn underwear and the mannequins are looking through microscopes. A man you find attractive walks up to you. You go to hold him and he becomes a puddle of phosphorescent semen on the floor. You walk over to one of the microscopes. You look through it. You see yourself being hurled naked onto subway tracks. You look through another microscope. You see nothing, but the moment your eye hits the lens you smell an attic unused for thirty years. A bat flies above your head smashing through the window. The shards of broken glass grow legs and eyes. They become insects. Then they become tiny replicas of you.

If the preceding seems an accurate account of your life these days, you already are an aesthetic surrealist. There is no need to contact us in order to join. The dues are armpits covered in worms, or doorknobs with fingers. The meetings are every second in your mind.

Pantoum for Dark Mornings

It's all just dumb show, anyway.
Our dreams, our getting through the day.
There's nothing on the scales to weigh.
My life's become a shadow play.

Our dreams, our getting through the day.
I keep alive by pills which beep.
My life's become a shadow play.
I want to do no more than sleep.

I keep alive by pills which beep.
A friend, he says I'm going to die.
I want to do no more than sleep.
My stupor sometimes lets me cry.

A friend, he says I'm going to die.
A foe, of course, in friend's disguise.
My stupor sometimes lets me cry.
But mostly I just close my eyes.

A foe, of course, in friend's disguise.
My sense of judgment spurts out blood.
But mostly I just close my eyes.
And lie here waiting for the flood.

My sense of judgment spurts out blood.
I want to die most every day.
And lie here waiting for the flood.
It's all just dumb show, anyway.

What Happens

What happens
do we become dust
do we dance with friends gone
awaiting friends to come
do we walk the tunnel of light
are our sins shown to us
in horrific detail
do we play and contemplate
is there music
do we plan our next adventure
do we wail and lament
do we scream
is there love
do we become part
of a whole
is there laughter
do we become swirls of light
of energy
is there thought
is the stench of decayed flesh
ever present
in our nostrils
is there memory
do we become etheric bodies
suffused with joy
do we become travelers
enlightened messengers
sent to soothe the sufferers
of other dimensions

do we see our former life
through noble eyes
do we become dust

Michael Lynch

Cry

Morning through a city garden widens
its swath. Shiny eyes of cinquefoil,
azure eyes of myosotis, bruised lobelia
refuse to blink. Intruders trapped in the cross-
stare harden, crumble into fine
dustings because our sympathies
will not adapt to sun and cinquefoil: our world
steel and concrete, oil and song.
We hoist our lives high over the drone
of traffic and screwing gulls, hoist bags
of soil to terraces at the setbacks; set out
cinquefoil, watch its leavings, count
its days. Some days we doze in the sun
and dream we too are cinquefoil or lobelia,
blowing and blanching without demur.
Then pneumocystis breaks.
We open our eyes to that skyline we incised
and know as a jet cuts through cloud that
cities are our gardens, with their stench
and contagion and rage, our memory, our
sepals that will not endure
these waves of dying friends
without a cry.

Late May. Toronto.

I.

This time of year the light hangs on so long
even our dinner parties gain
a Topic. Explain in five retorts
what so prolongs the day. Our latitude?
Longitude? Both—plus E.S.T.?
Besides the overflow of something to say
the days allow more time to say it in.
Guests linger over lettuce after dark.

This poem stops right there, but I'll amend
analogies, at risk (who ain't at risk?)
of contaminating the vinaigrette
(we're all contaminated).
A generation now is hanging on so long
we ask for explanations. Some live
into their thirties! Some, seven years
past diagnosis! Amazing cause for awe.

II.

A topographic explanation even here.
"One study showed" (such phrases herb
our salad dusks) that life expectancy
past diagnosis extended less in Los Angeles
than in a northern clime. More sun,

"the study showed," more viral replication.
"Who says it's not the freeways?" someone quips,
"or tinselled stress? or Cher's most recent dress?"

But multifactorialism's out of vogue
this month, and some defer to the new Sotadic
Zone with northern travels, wide-brimmed hats,
puce parasols, long sleeves. Tomorrow
when the Topic is the virus in the Yukon
no one connects. Parasols
hang on so long they too require an
explanation, a few more dinner parties.

III.

Recurrences aren't all bad. Today lilacs
burst on the city at 4 p.m.
Horse chestnuts, pink or white, strut
stuccoed head to toe with lit menorahs.
The Darwins fade, and the redbuds pale
to green, mere green, but still it's not yet
summer. A season, like its daylight,
lingers. It's only two weeks old.

I want it to stay. Spadina's summer stench,
the stench of the Expressway, the thousand
sausage sellers stationed everywhere downtown
to grill us with the stench of burning grease,
the stench of summer visitors in Aqua

Velva, of the body on the sidewalk, of new
provincial policies, swarming blackflies . . .
Let spring run through September, skip the sun.

IV.

Summer equals death. Even the sugar maple,
in this half-season, lives—little wads
of hint not blasted into symbol.
Nuance plays hide-and-seek in the alleys,
ideas not yet hardened into wisdom.
A youngster hardly twenty-three hangs on,
sustained by a hateful necessary tube
taped up his forehead, exiting down his nose,

so ancient no one visits anymore.
The forces of summer light will join
the forces of summer stench to dispatch
him. Hateful July. Hateful August.
It might be you (we're all contaminated)
so hold on to these lilacs while you can.
It won't be me. "The upside," said one queen,
"is you're too old, my dear, to die young."

V.

I planted a garden all in blue,
a folly. Why blue? Partly to escape
the bureaucracy's geraniums (nature's
nastiest red, natural as facelifts)
and marigolds, raw umbers with an equally raw
stench. Partly to resonate with Bessie,
Billie, and my foster home: the blues.

Today before the onset another motive's clear:
a garden which the sky can imitate,
cerulean, translucent, fresh as
flax, that airy spindly plant
with daily fresh deliveries of blue
to set the sky an example. Today's sky took
from flax and blue-white columbine:
blown with clouds like armfuls of mock orange.

VI.

Beside a rock the sysyrinchium, blue-eyed
grass, sees everything the small
can see. Linger through summer,
sysyrinchium. Miniatures may
win against the bludgeoning ahead,
delicacy outlive power.
Strength overweens. We
who yield to frailty do hang on

beyond prognostications. Look how my gripe
became a hymn to weakness! I lie abed
in what I call the garden bedroom
out of the sun but with full view of sky
and mock-orange clouds and bobbing
columbine and beds of forget-me-nots.
A time to gaze. A time to doze.
The sky, the garden, tapedeck, me: all blues.

VII.

Abed the body becomes a plant abed
where weakness bends in the wind but doesn't snap.
No broiling dogs in the garden
bedroom. The tube runs down the nose
and bruises blue, and the tape holding it
pinches, and one
gives up mobility one block at the time.

Each day new flax buds open, cast
glances around the sky-blue firmament,
fade, linger, waste. The sliding door,
all glass, becomes a lens where blues
convene from garden, patient, sky,
and Billie Holiday.
The door sees more than ever.
Sight, as summer strikes, shuts its blue eye.

Paul Mariah

Earth-Home

My people are earthy people, whose hair is coarsed-grey by
      familiar winds, whose hands are rough and massive
        farming
      the soil; the old wooden drawbucket is as familiar as
      the plows' grip or the weave of the loom, or the feel
      of the featherbed on cold winter nights, the same bed
      they were born in, made love in, and died in, as familiar
      as the grip force in holding the twig in witching for water,
      or the feel of the stump used as a worktable, or the handle
      of the hoe that knows the garden rows, or the lanterns
      thumbprint of day's labor,
Whose bodies are strong, well-weathered with pounds of sweat
      in the woof of the spin from the spinning wheel,
Whose faces are clayey and ruddy from oil of furrowed years,
      the lines running, curving toward the deathline, toward
      the virgin earth from whence they came,
Whose eyes are miracles of mother nature's sleep as though she
      were mothering them with savage woods, tame creeks,
        mossed
      trees, streams, eddies, sumac, hedgehogfruit and the path
      of the willow is found on the nightly walk. The solitude.
      These glens drew with them as childhoodroots, the hills
      where the white poplars dance on singing April nights,
      the gutted roads of winter's sudden thaw sidemarked by

sunkenfootprints gone to visit the neighbors to see
that all was well.

These familiar things, familiar as their own names: Rude, Izur
T.J., Mandy, Redus, so familiar they had forgotten their
real names. Izur was really Isaiah, but some young one
had such a slippery tongue he couldn't say it, hence
Isaiah became permanently Izur.
These earthy people are my people, the roots are from the same
ground, the ears keyed to whisperings of silent-things,
the scythe's sweep, the leap of animals at war, the clang
of the cowbell on distant dungpath, the sound of sugaring
down in seething syrup at canning time, the cherries,
wild strawberries, the albertas.
The sweetwild smell of honeysuckle inhaled deeply at dusk on
a nightly ritual, a walk to the graveside pasture to
lost daughter's marker who died from whooping cough
in '23
the marker is scented with new forgetmenots and daisies
picked on the wayside, this night, every night, by these
my people whose home is earth, whose home is my home,
whose dusted feet people the grave on a nightly ritual
with flowers, a bouquet nightly from these my people.
Now he is gone. She goes nightly with forgetmetnots and daisies
to cover them both. She has built a rose trellis above
their graves, so that all roots may grow together, her
Cyrus,
their daughter, their roots, with her trellis as an upward
guide. The glen dips behind the hills at sunset and she
comes home alone, in the dark, and no one sees her but

the owls whose eyes are moons, and the crickets who
    stop chirruping
when her feet comes too close and endanger their lives.
And no one sees her but the owls.

Scatterings

Mattress uprighted,
All belongings
Searched

Scattered, the box
Of paperclips
Spilled, strewn

All over concrete
Floor, stations
Of order

Disordered, guards
Waylay all
Objects.

Everything in cell
Has been touched
Handled

By huge hands,
Nothing is left
Untouched,

Sacred. Letters,
Emptied envelopes,
Green waterglass—

No thing is found.
All in cell has been
Shaken down.

The Spoon Ring

He had the silver
Handle of a spoon
Curled around
His finger.

His grandmother's
Silver,
A wedding present,
To preserve

The family crest.
The spoon ring
That I wear wings
Me back to prison.

The secret vows
Of prisoners
Exchange rings,
Silver contraband.

    (Whenever a spoon
    Is stolen from chow
    Line, frisks happen,
    Search for lost silver

    Either a shiv appears
    In some hidden corner
    Or a lover announces
    His bond, shows his hand.)

He did not know
The ritual of silver
As he showed me
His grandmother's ware.

A spoon, a wedding ring,
Crest of prison despair
That knows the ritual song
"To spoon the empty air."

Walls Breathe

It was so quiet you could hear

The walls breathe. It's almost mid
Night, I heard someone whisper
Down the galleywalk. Across were barred

Windows where you could see the licking
Flames. The matches lit as candles
Reflecting against the darkness outside
To light a candle in the memory of . . .

It was so quiet you could hear

Him fry. The metal cap placed
On his head. We were all there
Invisibly we circled the chamber
Where sacrament was a piece of flesh,
A peace of body. Silence to a brother

Reflecting windows and on the walls
Throughout the jail. The matches burned.
We remember the silence of the walls
The flame licking our fingers, our bones
We have to live with: you, a candle
In the window burning our minds.

We burned our fingers while they
Burned you and yours. A rite
Reflecting in the burning windows.

David Matias

Between Us

for Lenny

Two tiny blossoms fell from a tree, landing
between us as we strolled on the sidewalk.

And they made a noise. A noise no louder
than a thumb rubbing on fingertips.

My eyes caught their beauty for a second
as we made our way to the car.

Night clouds offered a moving moon
reflecting the white of those flowers,

pure against the cement's gray,
connected by a common stem.

Tell me it's a good omen we should stay together
and I will not suddenly reveal at the dinner table,

I don't know if I love you—
how wise is it *not* to follow my heart?

You will keep from answering back
that you've settled for me because

I'm better company than being alone.
The truths lie like petals on pavement.

Those blossoms will dry up, then be swept
by winds not tired of tossing little things about.

In time, with unspoken words, our bond deepens.
Doubt is too far under to be unburied.

With a glance, a look into each other's eyes,
we know the commitment between us.

I *grew* to love you and that was new for me.
If we have compromised, it's for the best.

You are older, I am ill, and we want
someone to hold at night. We want a history.

Tree blossoms might also fall in a puddle of rain,
keeping them afloat, alive much longer.

Concealed

My mother came 2000 miles to visit me Labor Day.
I know she talks about pain with only a few, maybe her husband.
She is cooking in my kitchen, she needs no book, no written
    recipe,
it's all in her head (*en la corazón*) the measurements are magic
and her loneliness I romanticize like dancing with a broomstick.

Early one morning she picks shells at low tide in front of my
    house,
Central Texas has no such wonders. She is 65, a retired school
teacher,
bending to touch wet sand. Barefoot, knocking her shoes near
    the door,
she asks what it means when the two halves of a shell are still
    closed.
It's alive, Mom. Like an offering she sets them on the brick landing.

I let her attend my therapy session, knowing she gets few
    chances
to hate death, to be angry at the rope tugging her only son.
Mom cries to my therapist, scared I don't tell her the truth
long distance over the phone when she asks, *How are you?*
She feels I protect her, keeping honesty hidden beneath my
    reply.

When I return to my home which faces the bay like courage,
I complain about the stinking mess of sun-heated sea clams,
now attracting a pester of fat flies. *Throw them away, Mom!*

She tosses the cream-white shells into the thicket of pine bushes
and smiles to herself. *Why did you keep them?* I bark.

I was hoping there might be a pearl inside.
I excuse myself to another room, my love for her at that moment
absorbed into a pillow. My disease has made her weak.
She claims she survives by getting strength from me.
She told my therapist, *I cannot believe how brave my son is,*

who instructed her to look at me and tell me. Purse at her feet,
Kleenex wadded in her palm, *I can't believe how brave you are.*
Mom, I often feel like a coward, frightened. But I need to hope
there is a treasure amongst this smell, this horror. It will open
    to us,
showing itself to be unearthly, a faith greater than all the ocean's
    jewels.

Fooling the Forsythia

Another friend died. Howard. He'll be missed.
He and all the others who have demystified death.

It's like having tea. I see it so often now.
And death is not a skeleton, it's much lovelier.

More like the stark branches cut in the month of March,
stuck in a glass brick filled with warm water,

looking simple and Japanese in the living room.
Lifeless the first few days. Until buds crack yellow.

A yellow that uncurls. Blossoms lively, unaware
of their own chopped ends or the cold winds

blowing outside, beautiful on the coffee table
and tricked into Spring. As I sit on the sofa staring,

sipping Camomile, watching snow turn into rain
turn into drizzle, I feel immortal for a moment.

A moment as brief as the silence when I drive under
an overpass in a storm. Surprised by the sudden

halt on the car's roof. Raindrops stop.
And for those few seconds, there's hope.

I change the water in the vase that has turned
foggy and stinks from the clear accumulated sap.

Bleeding, but bursting with color, these flowers
somehow blaze, with as much presence, as Howard.

James Merrill

Farewell Performance

for DK

Art. It cures affliction. As lights go down and
Maestro lifts his wand, the unfailing sea change
starts within us. Limber alembics once more
make of the common

lot a pure, brief gold. At the end our bravos
call them back, sweat-soldered and leotarded,
back, again back—anything not to face the
fact that it's over.

You are gone. You'd caught like a cold their airy
lust for essence. Now, in the furnace parched to
ten or twelve light handfuls, a mortal gravel
sifted through fingers,

coarse yet grayly glimmering sublimate of
palace days, Strauss, Sidney, the lover's plaintive
Can't we just be friends? which your breakfast phone call
clothed in amusement,

this is what we paddled a neighbor's dinghy
out to scatter—Peter who grasped the buoy,

I who held the box underwater, freeing
all it contained. Past

sunny, fluent soundings that gruel of selfhood
taking manlike shape for one last jeté on
ghostly—wait, ah!—point into darkness vanished.
High up, a gull's wings

clapped. The house lights (always supposing, caro,
Earth remains your house) at their brightest set the
scene for good: true colors, the sun-warm hand to
cover my wet one . . .

Back they come. How you would have loved it. We in
turn have risen. Pity and terror done with,
programs furled, lips parted, we jostle forward
eager to hail them,

more, to join the troupe—will a friend enroll us
one fine day? Strange, though. For up close their magic
self-destructs. Pale, dripping, with downcast eyes they've
seen where it led you.

Tony: Ending the Life

Let's die like Romans,
Since we have lived like Grecians.

—VOLPONE

Across the sea at Alexandria,
Shallow and glittering, a single shroud-
Shaped cloud had stolen, leaving as it paused
The underworld dilated, a wide pupil's
Downward shaft. The not-yet-to-be mined
Villa, a fortune of stone cards each summer
Less readable, more crushing, lay in wait
Beneath the blue-green sand of the sea floor.
Plump in schoolboy shorts, you peered and peered.
For wasn't youth like that—its deep charades
Revealed to us alone by passing shades?
But then years, too, would pass. And in the glow
Of what came next, the Alexandria
You brought to life would up and go:
Bars, beaches, British troops (so slim—yum yum!),
The parties above all. Contagious laughter,
Sparkle and hum and flow,
Saved you from weighty insights just below;
Till from another shore
(Folégandros, the western end of Crete)
Age, astonished, saw those heavy things
Lifted by tricky prisms into light,
Lifted like holy offerings,
Gemlike, disinterested,

Within the fleet
Reliquary of wave upon wave as it crested.

*

One year in Athens I let my beard grow.
The locals took it for a badge of grief.
Had someone died? Not yet, I tried to joke.
Of course beards came in every conceivable format—
Dapper, avuncular, deadbeat. . .
Mine warned of something creepier—uh-oh!
For over throat and lips had spread a doormat
On which to wipe filth brought in from the street.

Unfair! The boys were talkative and fun;
Far cleaner than my mind, after a bath.
Such episodes, when all was said and done,
Sweetened their reflective aftermath:
The denizens discovered in a dive
Relieved us (if not long or overmuch).
"Just see," the mirror breathed, "see who's alive,
Who hasn't forfeited the common touch,

The longing to lead everybody's life"
—Lifelong daydream of precisely those
Whom privilege or talent set apart:
How to atone for the achieved uniqueness?
By dying everybody's death, dear heart—
Saint, terrorist, fishwife. Stench that appalls.
Famines, machine guns, the Great Plague (your sickness),
Rending of garments, cries, mass burials.

I'd watched my beard sprout in the mirror's grave.
Mirrors *are* graves, as all can see:
Knew this emerging mask would outlast me,
Just as the life outlasts us, that we led . . .
And then one evening, off it came. No more
Visions of the deep. These lines behave
As if we were already gone—not so!
Although of course each time's a closer shave.

One New Year's Eve, on midnight's razor stroke,
Kisses, a round of whiskies. You then drew
Forth from your pocket a brightness, that season's new
Two drachma piece, I fancied, taking the joke
—But no. Proud of your gift, you warned: "Don't leave
The barman this. Look twice." My double take
Lit on a grave young fourteen-carat queen
In profile. Heavens preserve us! and long live

Orbits of Majesty whereby her solar
Metal sets the standard. (A certain five-dollar
Piece, redeemed for paper—astute maneuver—
Taught me from then on: don't trust Presidents.)
Here it buys real estate. From the packed bus's
Racket and reek a newly-struck face glints
No increment of doubt or fear debases.
Speaking of heavens, Maria, a prime mover

In ours, one winter twilight telephoned:
Not for you to see her so far gone,

But to pick up, inside the unlatched door,
A satchel for safekeeping. *Done and done,*
You called from home to say. But such a weight,
Who lifted it? No one. She'd had to kick,
Inch by inch, your legacy down the hall,
The heavy bag of gold, her setting sun.

*

The sea is dark here at day's end
And the moon gaunt, half-dead
Like an old woman—like Madame Curie
Above her vats of pitchblende
Stirred dawn to dusk religiously
Out in the freezing garden shed.

It is a boot camp large and stark
To which you will be going.
Wave upon wave of you. The halls are crowded,
Unlit, the ceiling fixtures shrouded.
Advancing through the crush, the matriarch
Holds something up, mysteriously glowing.

Fruit of her dream and labor, see, it's here
(See to how scarred her fingertips):
The elemental sliver
Of matter heading for its own eclipse
And ours—this "lumière de l'avenir"
Passed hand to hand with a faint shiver:

Light that confutes the noonday blaze.
A cool uncanny blue streams from her vial,
Bathing the disppearers
Who asked no better than to gaze and gaze . . .
Too soon your own turn came. Denial
No longer fogged the mirrors.

You stumbled forth into the glare—
Blood-red ribbon where you'd struck your face.
Pills washed down with ouzo hadn't worked.
Now while the whole street buzzed and lurked
The paramedics left you there,
Returning costumed for a walk in Space.

The nurse thrust forms at you to sign,
Then flung away her tainted pen
. . . Lie back now in that heat
Older than Time, whose golden regimen
Still makes the palm grown tall and the date sweet . . .
Come, a last sip of wine.

Lie back. Over the sea
Sweeps, faint at first, the harpist's chord.
Purple with mourning, the royal barge gasps nearer.
Is it a test? a triumph? No more terror:
How did your namesake, lovesick Antony,
Meet the end? By falling on his sword

—A story in Plutarch
The plump boy knew from History class.
Slowly the room grows dark.

Stavro who's been reading you the news
Turns on a nightlight. No more views.
Just your head, nodding off in windowglass

Vol. XLIV, No. 3

Room set at infrared,
Mind at ultraviolet,
Organisms ever stranger,
Hallucinated on the slide, fluoresce:

Chains of gold tinsel, baubles of green fire
For the arterial branches—
Here at *Microcosmics Illustrated*, why,
Christmas goes on all year!

Defenseless, the patrician cells await
Invasion by barbaric viruses,
Another sack or Rome.
A new age. Everything we dread.

Dread? It crows for joy in the manger.
Joy? The tree sparkles on which it will die.

Paul Monette

The Bee-Eater

for Carol Muske

We walk on air, Watson.
—SYLVIA PLATH

The killer bees—Africanized—have reached San Diego
and I got a C– in Elementary Sci.
New evidence every day that I wasted my youth
on English Lit. That is, I don't know shit
about pollination or why bugs are our friends.
Not that I haven't followed them north
year by year, valley by valley, bearing
the beaded sungod of El Dorado,
the dewdrop gleam of the eagle priests
who heal by sting and pistil. How many times
have I bolted awake with a guilty terror—
the swarm upon me, roaring like a 747.
Once even dreamed I was eating them
like a mouthful of blackberries

                                taste of

gunmetal and caramel

                        couldn't scream

through the foam of pain

                    A veritable
balloon-man all through my tenth summer, I was
the bees' bullseye. The whole hive courted me—
yellowjackets, blue-bellied hornets, furry
bumbles, two-inch wasps. I drew them like
a rotten plum. By August I was on a steroid
drip. Next year they let me be, and the next
and the next, but you never lose the fear
of buzzing
                    roses are never the same
                                        nor sweets
nor syrup nor even soap. You wash with
oatmeal, chew garlic, dress gray, screen
callers, wander only after dark—

Now I know how an allergy works:
life gives you an A in your own disease.
You take a little venom at a time
and soon you purr with tolerance. Say one
a day, stinger applied directly to the tongue
or sucked like a quivering lozenge.
Self-treatment you'll say is risky:
Jack London OD'd at 40, needling
himself for tropical fevers, and all
the wolves in Yellowknife howled
at the moon in grief
                    but no entomologists

Addiction may occur. Look, the doctors
don't know shit either. The bee-men
got their timetable wrong, and here I am,
not immune enough. If I don't start eating now
they'll be here, covering the house
like a pear tree. Measure my days
by sting if I have to. It's August,
the garden is moaning, we have no
winter to hide in. So bring on the just
desserts, the honey-domed, the dream-
candy kamikaze panacea kiss of death.

Oh bees my bees, come take me.

Here

everything extraneous has burned away
this is how burning feels in the fall
of the final year not like leaves in a blue
October but as if the skin were a paper lantern
full of trapped moths beating their fired wings
and yet I can lie on this hill just above you
a foot beside where I will lie myself
soon soon and for all the wrack and blubber
feel still how we were warriors when the
merest morning sun in the garden was a
kingdom after Room 1010 war is not all

death it turns out war is what little
thing you hold on to refugeed and far from home
oh sweetie will you please forgive me this
that every time I opened a box of anything
Glad Bags One-A-Days KINGSIZE was
the worst I'd think will you still be here
when the box is empty Rog Rog who will
play boy with me now that I bucket with tears
through it all when I'd cling beside you sobbing
you'd shrug it off with the quietest *I'm still
here* I have your watch in the top drawer
which I don't dare wear yet help me please
the boxes grocery home day after day
the junk that keeps men spotless but it doesn't
matter now how long they last or I
the day has taken you with it and all
there is now is burning dark the only green
is up by the grave and this little thing
of telling the hill I'm here oh I'm here

Your Sightless Days

Blind eyes could blaze like meteors and be gay
—DYLAN THOMAS

I remember clearly deciding not to see
anymore myself this out of sheer protest
or only see what I could tell you the whole of
art was out so was anything new the buff
hillside gone to grass was just our speed
but of course I was always minimizing
as if to say there's nothing to see today
it's the same old thing Rog sycamore's bare
park full of Seurats but hey feel that breeze
and knowing how clear Aegean blue your eyes were
please I know what I watched go out but even
when it struck us down blacked our windows
like an air raid even then your glimmering half
sight was so seductive *What do you see*
I'd ask you coaxing every street sign like
they were glyphs off a ruined temple night
would fall you'd frown *Are the lights on Paul*
and tear my heart all the Bette Davis lines
out to get us but oh my dearest every one
was on spots flashes searches long white tubes
like the swords in *Star Wars* candlepower fit
for a Byzantine saint and still so dim the dark
so jealous of life and then out of nowhere
a neon day of LA sun we're out strolling
you stop peer impish intent as a hawk

and say *I see you* just like that and THEN
I toss my blinders and drink the world like water
till the next dark up and down for half a year
the left one gone in April overnight
two millimeters on the right side saved
and we fought for those that knife of light
and beaten ground raging for day like the
Warsaw ghetto all summer long I dripped
your veins at 4 and midnight watching every
drop as if it was sight itself so did we
win did we lose you died with the barest
shadows oh I know but even then we hoped
a cataract laser might give us a glint
would not see night as the way of the world
and what have I seen since your blindness my
love just that my love requires no eyes so
why am I tapping this thin white cane of outrage
through crowds of sighted fools the pointless trees
and the awful dusk unlifting some few colors
bright as razor blades trying to make me look
I'm shut tight Oedipus-old leave me alone
I have somehow gotten it all wrong because
when you were the blackest blind you laughed *laughed*
groped your way and stared the noon sun down
How are you jerks would ask *Read Job* you'd say
a gleam in every good hour pulling out puns
and Benny jokes and fighting to read the charts
knowing the worst had fallen you'd hoot on the phone
and wrestle the dog so the summer was still
the summer Rog see how you saw us through

Cookie Mueller

The Mystery of Tap Water

Julie lost her mind one day, just like that. Well, really, it had taken two weeks to lose it completely. She had always been eccentric, but now she was past that. She believed very strongly in the principle, You are what you eat, so she experimented with water. She drank it—no food, no juice, just water—for two weeks. She was convinced that since she would be only water she could disappear at will.

I saw her the night before she disappeared and she was pretty lucid. She told me that she had lived forever, that she would never die, and since she was all water she must have been the iceberg that sank the *Titanic*, the heavy water used in making the hydrogen bomb, the basic element used with Kool-Aid in Jonestown, Guyana.

"I feel very guilty," she said.

Her last words before she left were: "When you see a gushing fountain, I'll be there. When you sip a glass of ice water, I'll be there. When there's a torrential downpour, a cloudburst, a flood, a blizzard, a lawn sprinkler, that's me."

"Okay," I smiled, "I'll look for you."

No one ever saw her again.

"Oh, she's so elusive," everyone said, "She'll turn up sooner or later in some mental hospital."

But she never did.

I know it's absurd and ridiculous, but now whenever I take a bath I see Julie pouring out of the faucet, and I begin to wonder just how many other odd people and complete strangers are in the bathtub floating around with me.

Which Came First?

It was over breakfast at the Chuck Wagon Bistro that Sarah mentioned that she couldn't eat eggs in the morning in her own kitchen. It was something that had haunted her for many years, since she had left her parents' home, in fact.

"Even the idea makes me nauseous," she said.

"Even over-scrambled?" her friend Vera asked.

"Actually, I can eat hard-boiled eggs in the afternoon at home. Maybe it has something to do with my disgusting cookware. I need new cookware."

Sarah was not the sort of person who talked about home appliances. But Vera, a friend of more than seventeen years, was that sort of person. Sarah saw Vera rarely; she never knew quite what to talk about with her. She was always so concerned with the banality of kitchen minutiae.

Suddenly Vera said something that was so unVera-like.

"I think I know why you can't eat eggs at home. It's because eggs are so congenitally girlie," Vera said, and Sarah knew she was right, but her choice of words was so uncharacteristic that Sarah laughed. Vera had never made Sarah laugh in all the years she'd known her.

"Also, I read that when you crack open an egg and drop it into the hot oil, it sends out agony vibrations and that traumatizes any house plants that are near. They go into some sort of vegetable shock," Vera added.

Now, coming from someone else, this would have been very matter-of-fact, but from Vera it was an eye-opener.

Sure, Sarah certainly knew all about the sensitivity of plants; she had read *The Private Lives of House Plants* and also the explosive piece on plants in the *Atlantis, Lemuria and Mount Shasta Journal*. It was about how scientists wired plants for their electro-psychic-vibration reaction to Beethoven, household violence, and slicing of vegetables. It was clearly proven that plants were highly sympathetic.

"Vera, I never thought you were interested in things like this."

"Well, I haven't seen you in a year, Sarah. I've changed. Six months ago I was living on Jane Sillman's ashram farm. I learned a lot there."

There was a grand silence, broken only by the slosh of a sunnyside's clear mucus, which accidentally slithered off Sarah's suspended fork and back onto the plate.

"The famous Lesbian Occult Ranch?" Sarah asked. Was this really Vera?

"It's called the Feminist Life Force Farm," Vera corrected. "I'm experimenting with other meaningful relationships outside of heterosexual ones. You should know all this; your relationship with Janet is great, isn't it?"

A subway train went by under the restaurant. The table knocked the way it would at a séance.

"Well, yes, but . . ." How could she tell Vera that having a great relationship with a woman is the same as having a great relationship with a man?

At home Sarah thought about Vera. Miracles never cease. Perhaps Vera was experiencing the famous mid-life crisis. Maybe she was having a mind-expanding revelation. A spiritual rebirth? Maybe she even saw auras and talked about third eyes and Beings of Light with the ashram fems. Whatever the reason, Vera was happier.

But it was such a staggering turn. Vera had been a jaundiced homemaker—baloney sandwiches and iced tea at noon, the hum of her vacuum cleaner was music to her ears.

That night Sarah had a dream about the eggs in her refrigerator. Those eggs had been there for a long time. Obviously, she felt some deep-seated guilt about shunning them. In the dream she opened her refrigerator and each egg was shining with a blue light. The eggs then started to move, then hatch. The refrigerator somehow had incubated them.

Out of each egg came a full feathered sparrow. All twelve flew into the kitchen. The phone rang but she couldn't locate it amid all the fluttering birds.

Finally she found it and told the person on the phone that there were birds everywhere. But then she realized that there were no birds and the person on the phone was real and it had been a dream.

The person on the phone was Vera.

"I just called to tell you how much I enjoyed breakfast yesterday," Vera said, and she also told her that she was going away on an extended fishing trip with her girlfriend, a new lover.

"That's wonderful, Vera," Sarah said, and tried to imagine Vera baiting a hook.

Sarah was sure that this night she would dream about the frozen Mrs. Paul's fish sticks that had been in her freezer for three months.

For an old friend, would one dream any less?

J. M. Regan

In the Confessional

At my first town meeting
on the bare and veiled receiving ward
where I sat shouting
at the uncaring wall—*rape kill die*—
the other inmates cowered
the way I cringe from flowers, and the blue sky.
Then they all thanked me for sharing.

That visiting hour I woke up and saw,
like waking to a nightmare,
my hour-of-my-death mother—
beak and feather,
hawk's-eye, bloody claw.
This was stuff no dream was made on.
I screamed and ran.

(My dreams are full of
flash, and fire, and thrashing love
with pricks thick
as my neck.
They balloon and enter
like the body of the lake
finally ballooned into my millstoned father.)

For breakfast I'd eat thorazine.
That magnetic thorazine!

My head and torso
twisted twisted toward the east
as though in quest of Xst
and forced, like the morning glory,
to shrivel at the first light.

Elavil was helpful too.
I never got bored.
When I'd open my book, each word
untwirled from the sentences.
I'd watch them twinkle into the distances,
lyrical as birds of happiness.
Neither did I miss my libido.

I'd unload on my doctor.
She was cold, controlled, and spoke in codes,
like a computer.
She dismissed all my trespasses.
Sins vicious as tetrapods!
For my penance I'd agree to eat supper,
and once my soul'd snapped shut as the jaws on the lioness,

my brain soon grew sane as God.
Freed of grief and old leafages,
my two feet re-rooted.
My fired – *oh orange!* – wings burned to ashes.
Now I'm steady as iron
in my deaf-mute aloof cocoon.
I am the dead.

Nothing, however, shall be left unsaid.

Partial Luetic History of an Individual at Risk

In the Downtown Tombs of long long ago
    I learned how
to roll tobacco,
and eat stew with my fingers
    like a Hindu,
and survive getting raped all day by murderers.
In return I earned an eternally positive sera,

and became a natural host, a host-plant
    the drowned feed from,
a stand in the water my doctor flails
    the seed-pods from—
with his polyclinic hands and seas of hair
    I nearly disappear under,
how I sprout and flower flower
for my sky-blue and Mediterranean doctor.

He sneaks looks at me like a dirty picture.
When I was small and caught men watching me like that,
I thought they hated me.
But now I'm big and think better.
I think I'm protected.

It's not all *bad, it's not* all *bad,*
he keeps promising—
as though *good* or *bad* had a single thing
    to do with it!—
and, *Did I hurt you?*—the pick in the duct.
I don't know.

Are you still suicidal?—prob-
   ing my swollen groin.
It's an option, doc.
While the cringing vein, sick of invasion,
reluctant to give up more blood,
drips drips drips into the rubber tube.

My Jewish doctor loves me truer,
sitting rigid at the bare Care Center
   like a gaunt tree,
and the air of a bored whore,
one eye on her watch,
one hand in her snatch,

one fact a nest of snakes to shock
   me into shape—
inescapably stable, like iron.
They held a razor to my neck.
The world, she says, *is full of irritation.*
Our hour's up.

Two decades later now I've got
   stigmata,
I'm going holy:
tongue and palate cancers, gummatous
   change
engage my way of tasting, tasting, my way
   with speech.
It's grown unruly.

It's exploding my bones.
Find me a spontaneous cure! the kind
    that purifies the lives of saints
and drives the sun to leave its prints
in every leaf, and each brief bird,
and even in the marrows of the stones.

Richard Ronan

A Lady in a Northern Province

Colorless morning:
      my sleeves are weighted
with waxlike creatures of ice
          —fish, dogs, a white-
          blooded deer—

a thin winter,
      wide with your absence.

I have a carp frozen
      in a wheel of clear ice,
its orange veils of fire open,
its gold eyes wet and hard;
        for two days
      it has stood on a tile
      before my pallet,
         unmelting.

Yes, I love you most in this trial
        of winter;
love you also when the white goat
        looks at me,
with sudden intelligence, compassion.
I love you at the pool's edge
      that bears in frosted mud

the print of your feet,
                your palm, your hip.

In your absence
I've built a tight fire
                which burns like the black wheel
                        in a tiger's eye.

I feed it coal
I feed it my hair, strand by strand,
                        so that you return whole
                        and undamaged
                bearing a heart that is still mine.

Love Among Lepers

First, for kindness, we must assume the dark;
it is not right to see this. Not outright, perhaps not even inwardly.
Things often wound the eye & remain like picks of glass,
     wounding again,
tearing again through the recent scabbing of the thing seen &
     seen again,
a red dream recurring.
Darkness then. And in it wordlessness.
Let us be strict in this, for we can never know our partner's
latest turn of unhealth, if he has, since last loved, lost a lip
& is now imperfect of any answer, even to our softest, sweet word.

No, kinder not to speak at all, even if we still can.
Besides, what is there to say? What framing, what bodying
forth in speech can you or I give this slow process,
the gradual cessation of systems. Pieces & pieces, feelings
in the loving arm forgetting themselves by bits,
losing the long-assumed narration that has kept it in its shape
& in its kind of sentence so long.
The corrosion of vessels, of living nerve confused
as if with ash, ash of a forest burnt black upstream,
one that leapt carbonized & howling into the cooling blood?
How could we ask with any tenderness after the damage upriver,
the cellular losses, the soldiery in the blackened slough,
the muck driving down from the minute frontiers of wilderness,
from the high stairway, from the pith of the heart,
flowing from trickles to lava runs, a nutrient stew,
poison now, alpha gone all omega, the horror
we must watch even in darkness & await.

No, the etiquette, though broken so often with sobbing,
must be silence: at least we must not speak.
Any word can run mad with itself, and with evisceration of itself
& there is no word for living through this, there is no word for
     witnessing
our beloved fail piecemeal, no word to speak the itch
inside the fingers to be off, candle wax thinning to the bone-wick,
no word conveying the centering toward a more & more
essential which is itself essential to nothing & no one
but ourselves, in useless love, in unsupporting darkness, tongues
                    numb and as slow as sick dogs.

Darkness in the room. Darkness in the mind, the heart & spirit
the clean table, the finger like a glass pen drawing us in contours
    of light.
Eyes. Yours. Skin. Your skin,
misted as if by the spray of luminous surf,
salty & damp as sweat, your abrupt vigor, the shudders
& jolts from where you sat once upon me & reeled dizzy into
selflessness—I see it with the darkened eye
& touch you, still whole enough to read you,
to have always read you & beyond you & through you into you
& into that which was divine, that to which you gave flesh,
this radiance that cannot still our pain.
Is there still this, in the life-worn husks we've weathered into?
remnants of it embering of our deep and volatile love,
some fossil of a phoenix to redeem what has come to be,
with what had once been? Oh, what a wet planet we were,
made half of great fire and how we descend the stairs,
mountains melting into slag-laden fumes, iron poured
on the hot sea, the sea boiled off into a brief power
of thunderheads, spewing a molten rain onto nothing remaining,
but this: remembered passion, the distant passion.
We are the things of such things that see nothing in our pain.

Here, we've forgotten again our meager impulse toward love,
we fall onto softened shoulders. You sob.
I am too tired to weep. We lose the thought of what we meant
to do together.

Beloved, I love you & there is no god.
Oh, I love you and there is no hope.
Look how we are still so hungry for each other

& still we will not live.

The linens clenched in your white fists as you sit up, dark,

a felt shape that I cannot see & you are sounding

a long sharpened EEEEEEEE in the throat, far off,

as if far off, the knife cutting another pound,

another god-hating, faith-rotten day of gristle & ash.

And then it is me—EEEEEEE—again and I see the bloodless,

open-mouthed loss of you. Again.

And again I close your imperfect eyes because again

they are left half open & no one to stare through them,

again the autumn sunlight outside & your face no longer yours.

Oh what was it I was? Where is he I loved?

The wind, the sun

The wind EEEEEEEE

and tell me again,

why is it we live to see such as this again?

Redwoods

I.

the thousand trunks of the

redwoods go up toward a

centre: it is a harbour of

them   each mast sheeted

out with leaves and needles

fronds and the nets of spiders:

they are ships yearning at
their ropes   yearning out of
their roots for the centre
which is the flame-sun above

harboured like this they list
impatiently creaking
waiting for wind   the spiders
take in insects like fish
they also net thin shafts of
light that fall to the redwood
floor   they rush out when
a catch tugs on the silk
as happy as if they'd gathered
meteors   as if they'd caught
a star

II.

young redwoods often grow
out of the burnt-out hollows
of more venerable trees—
these fallen fifty years
before to fire   the black ring
at the base that was the old
tree's footing nourishes the
young trees with its carbon
and with its memory of an
air six-hundred feet above

the young trees race up
also to the centre   making
a vault   a space that points
utterly at the sun: they
smell the fire both above
and below: they see a
crown above as brilliant
as the crown they suck below
is black: they follow

III.

the monastery at tassajara
was said to be imperiled
for six days   as the land-
fire raged out of control.
it melted rock in a heat
so great it might have been
the surface of the sun—
it was at least a novice
of the sun suddenly breathing
fire on the mountain.
the monks sent the children
away   released the goats
and hitched their skirts
above the smoke   they
swung axes into the thick
trunks surrounding the home
and with the fire-workers
made a wide avenue around

themselves   they hung the
roof with wet blankets
wet the floors   the supporting
timbers: everything was
centered on the fire and for
the fire   all came into focus
for the fire

but tonight begins a new age
an owl will appear on the
carbon branch of a cypress
and stare from that perch that
is as lovely as coral and as
dead   the owl will see the
burnt bracken pointing its
remnant at the moon   it will
hear the low wind and it will
cry: on! on! build toward
the lord above!

Soe

You step from the shower,
the water beaded,
worked into ringlets down a tight
oiled skin: our lives
are running beside each other
like vines climbing themselves,
reaching up the bed,
beneath the breakfast table,
shared hands/mouth/hair.
There is a rooted part of us.
We are an event continuing
before our own eyes.

I think of gods
because of you,
now standing in the doorway,
lighted by white walls and dampness:
I think that they are beautiful, of course,
skins like dolphins or seals spinning
through water—
and that they are flesh,
that they live only as flesh,
among us, as us,
every morning rubbing the steam
from the mirror in the bathroom,
squinting at their jaws:
gods.

Soe: it means the place of man
in the line from earth to heaven;
also, the purpose of a man:
to be the eyes and ears of heaven,
the blood of earth, mouth of god, the flesh
shining before a speechless tongue
of clay.
It is today your task to arrive, moist,
tossing rain like a terrier;
mine to see it occur
in our tangle of time,
to say that it is here,
now, like this.

All day long I write this,
drinking the thin waters
that gather on your spine,
mouth of god, tongue of man.

The Woman Who Kept the Boy Who Kept Cats

The sex over and done, we were, more or less,
      a charcoal ladder
         of coals.
When the breeze blew, his back glimmered up,
an orange rash of stars,
           mean-eyed in the dark,
      a thousand cats awakened in the future
      by the slit-eyed scent of rain.

We'd come to the cliffs again,
         leapt at each other's thighs
      and, in free fall, infinite and deep fall,
      committed again our infinite disregard
         for living long.
      Bones rung, singing like hammerheads
      struck on pads, muscle
              harder than bone,
      on skin stuck with the garment of tongues
           and juices.

And this time we broke the face
         of that wall of friends within,
      so fearful of our well-being,
         our audience of aunts;
he chewed my hard nipples raw,
      splintered a hip
         climbing on, in and out of me.
Then it went quick past pain,
      the fast male rush at the white circle

where pain lays out her silks
to be stolen or stained;
            then this
                  long, long apocalypse
        where I'm wondering wide, wondering down:
          how could I have opened his back
like that with my fingers,
      so that it looks like a bird
      had dug there, a dog
after the ass-end scent of his heart,
         and not have *known* it,
      neither he nor I,
so seized or suspended were we, so fire-mouthed.

Before he fell asleep between my legs,
        and became this impossible weight
    pulled by some magnet whose line runs from his thick
      body
          though mine to the center of a molten earth,
            he said to my belly
            that he'd kept cats
            as a boy
       in milk boxes, a dovecote, bags sometimes;

    that he and his dimwit brother hunted them,
    lured them with cream and slabs of fish
    and then put them inside
    where they went wild with gut yowling
       and vicious hisses,

just to see them change, hear them change
from slow paws and pussies to a knot of claws
                and piss-white hatred,
        to sit quite close beside them while they tried
        to cut out his eyes,
                to soft-talk them
                some sweet trash and tell them
                that he loved them.

Assotto Saint

Heaven in Hell

for counsel wright

there stood a blue-eyed booted brute
chaps cap smile of steel
the kind we knelt to in backrooms
on your third anniversary
in remembrance i slaved
headful of poppers
mouthful of cum
soulful of heaven
may i never know
that hellfire of fevers
with which your breath burned
out

Lord Have Mercy

manacled on a cross of purple
leather pillows puffed with lamentations
buffed by the sweat of strapped angels
straddled through infernal nights of rites
savage souls salvaged
in the flicker of a votive candles-circle
i watched baldhead gabriel genuflect
frail naked freckled like a leopard
the morning after
he had worn his whiteness best in black
armored crusader in rhythm
"i don't remember
your name" his cruel lips curled
"it doesn't matter i have
a lover" i sighed unmasked
in blessed remission
like a priest he kissed
then uncuffed my feet

Souvenir

tracing back dirt roads
i wanted to write a happy carefree poem
for my country

turquoise skies
amethyst mountains
emerald oceans
acres upon acres of sugar cane
miles upon miles of rice fields
thousands upon thousands of coconut trees
all shimmering in the seas' breeze
drumbeats that strike thunderclaps
pipe-puffing ladies in colorful dresses
candle-stiff under baskets
of guavas mangos papayas
ripe with sweetness

i wanted to write a happy carefree poem
for my childhood
lost too fast thirteen years ago
somewhere in the air
between port-au-prince & new york city
but i'm left bereft
by faces with no trace of smiles
eyes without vision

in postcards
haiti is the pearl of the islands
hallmark trick

in 1983
haiti is a cemetery

streets packed with zombies
souls sold to baby doc
who boogies in palais national
like baron samedi
even the banda lost its rhythm

skinny carrefour hustlers
tickle their dicks
for those few tourists
who still dare
ensnared by magic

every other woman's belly is laden
with another baby
every other man's head is laden
with another figurine to sculpt
canvas to paint
tap-tap to drive

"bon dié bon oui" preaches the priest
who carries a camera
records confessions
for loups-garous tontons macoute
the land is parched
with ash of infected swine
everywhere hands stretch out of time
to anyone
for anything

Paul Schmidt

Going Through Customs

Anything of value to declare?
she says, and I want to start snickering,
hey, I'm a poet,
anything I declare is of value.
She asks me again and I try to be modest,
but the fact is I'm stumped. I mean,
what have I got?

All around me are people unpacking their bring-backs
from Greece—the blankets and bracelets,
the beads and the pots—same kind of stuff
we sold to the Indians here once.
And then there's the shamefaced look
on the face of a fat man holding a vase
with two grinning satyrs going at it.
What I've got is a couple of sponges
as presents, stiff and awkwardly stuffed
in a suitcase corner, also a head full of images,
not Instamatic, most of them blurred.

It wasn't so much what I saw, I understand now,
as things I heard. A shout, the cicadas, a song,
a donkey braying at dawn, the rattle of pebbles
as small waves beat on a beach.

And I remember a word: *níhta*,
said by a woman in black beside the road.
It was Greek to me, almost unintelligible
in the breeze that moved in the pine trees,
and overhead the pines and the sky
erased each other, and below the road
the sea was losing its light.

I can't say I heard the sea darken
the way I heard those beach pebbles rattle,
but what I heard stayed in my head,
and a long time later lying in a bathtub
I drop in a sponge (I decided to keep one
myself) and it touches the water and darkens
with something I swear is a sound.

The sponge thickens slowly, sinks out of sight.
I understand then that *níhta* means night.

The Operation

(*"... circumcised at six*
by mother and grandmother
on the dining room table ...")

October. It was all golden, full of sunlight
an dapple smell, and I still remember the poem
she made me learn, by Helen Hunt Jackson.
A day when I might have floated, might have opened
my mouth in the sunlight and spoken pure Greek.

Nobody's fear has power over bright weather,
ever. It pours in everywhere, picks out
the polish on woodwork and windows,
grandmother's doing. It even shines on a knife set
out on the dining room table, casting a shadow.

I'm a boy in the kitchen learning to cook by breaking
eggs in a pan and watching liquid stiffen;
that all eggs don't make chickens,
that infertility feeds, that lack of accomplishment
is a dish in its own right—that's part of the lesson.

I learn that something soft can harden,
that heat, which hurts, re-forms, refines. My eyes
shine, though that same heat would fry them
too, without protection. But I still had lots
to learn about protection, and hardness, and heat.

In the bathroom my sister stares at her breast in the mirror.
It stiffens too. Her hot hand kneads it, it rises
like the lumps of dough on the stove, grandmother's loaves.
The yeast of wildness works inside her already,
unseen by the guardian angel on her bedroom wall.

In an upstairs room my mother moves her hands.
Her ring is platinum, with one small diamond missing.
She opens a drawer, it is full of snakes. They lie
in slick loops, rustling among forbidden novels
she thinks she's hidden beneath folded underwear.

She reads in secret, but never learned the lesson
secrecy teaches: no one sees you when you're all alone.
The Virgin's feet on the serpent's head was all
the model she had; she could not hear beyond
the cold rattle of this, her coiled Christendom.

Father on his way to work stops, he wonders
if he's forgotten something. He kicks some asters,
wishing he'd trimmed them weeks ago. Neat,
he wants everything neat, and it isn't, and that
is the reason his hands are always shaking.

In the garage he lets the motor idle, and for a moment
dreams of shutting the doors and staying there
forgetting the bleak contrivances of a life
full of broken tools. He could bubble forever
in a puddle of oblivion. But he goes to work instead.

My grandmother walks down the stairs.
Sunlight from the window above the landing
licks her face. Her dress is black. She takes
each step deliberately, with sense of wonder
at what can be accomplished on a day like this.

Her look and her feeling are greater and grander
than folds of clean linen or high mass at Assumption,
something tremendous that blows out of time, from beyond
the Irish hills. She keeps hearing voices of angels,
the unsexed murmur of selfless devotion to God.

The boy in the kitchen thinks to himself:
if I trust the power of heat and learn
the consequences, why should I fear
anything at all? Who needs protection?
He tilts the pan, and the grease catches fire.

And all at once the car engine dies,
the drawer in the bedroom closes, grandmother pauses
on the landing and sister covers her breast, as a pillar
of fire bursts from the kitchen right through the roof,
a great glowing tower of perfect heat!

Then came the stillness of catastrophe.
They all went rushing outside and looked up,
hoping as always for a miracle, but all they saw
was a minor vision, a scared and petulant child
standing in a foliage of flames, who said:

"I never wanted this transfiguration,
this role of spiteful screamer unable to go
or stay. I would have gone, but I'm perverse.
You cannot cut me off so easily. I'll hang
around your house forever now, like a sour smell.

I'll infest your attic and moulder your heirlooms,
your framed diplomas, and the photo of Uncle Alfred
in the only boat the family ever owned.
I will hide little bottles in Christmas stockings
and turns your grandsons from baseball to booze.

I am the fingers of your amputated hands,
the early morning fear that knots your vitals,
the ache in your organs long after the hysterectomy,
the thought of cancer growing in your gut
that all your whiskey evenings cannot put out.

Remember me." Then the fire went out. I opened
my mouth to scream, but nothing came. A white
cloth covered my face with the toppling odor
of chloroform. A mess of membranes, knives and bloody
bandages. And bread at that table still tastes the same.

For years I said nothing. October grew darker
and all knives were always dull, whatever
the weather. How could I know they had cut out my tongue
as well, left me a grafted stump, and out of it
only now something sprouts, and begins to burn?

Jack Sharpless

The Maid

Wrung
laundry
hangs
from
fragrant
plum
boughs.

I sit on
the grassy
riverbank,

pretending
not to wait
for you
to coax me
beneath
billowing
folds.

The Potter

A really fine thing,
smashed to pieces.

what once
poured tea
with such refined
grace and meaning
for a thousand years,

swept to the floor
with a crash.

After a
single shock,
not a roof tile
in the district
remained intact.

The Suicide

"Lastly, do I vow
that my eyes desire you
above all things."

The blood crept out
past her fingertips.

One-hundred
lustrous butterflies
splayed lifeless
on an Autumn pond.

Soon,
it would be Winter.

The Widow

Slept uneasily
in the heat
of my rooms,

woke damp and
tangled with dreams
in the dark.

I ventured out
into the garden's
blue-jade moonlight.

Jasmine once again
incenses
late summer nights,

though no trace of
your smoky fragrance
rekindles these haunts.

Thought I saw
cities afire
on the horizon.

The Witness

The lacquer
of evening
glowed
on every surface.

Dragons of fire
leapt over the old
Tartar City.

Claws of flame
tore at the
populace's belly.

Bright jaws
devoured
the granaries
in a single bite.

Reginald Shepherd

Antibody

I've heard that blood will always tell:
tell me then, antigen, declining white cell count
answer, who wouldn't die for beauty
if he could? Microbe of mine, you don't have me
in mind. (The man fan-dancing from 1978
hit me with a feather's edge across the face, ghost
of a kiss. It burned.) Men who have paid
their brilliant bodies for soul's desire, a night
or hour, fifteen minutes of skin brushed against
bright skin, burn down to smoke and cinders
shaken over backyard gardens, charred
bone bits sieved out over water. The flat earth
loves them even contaminated, turned over
for no one's spring. Iris and gentian
spring up like blue flames, discard those parts
more perishable: lips, penises, testicles,
a lick of semen on the tongue, and other things
in the vicinity of sex. Up and down the sidewalk
stroll local gods (see also: saunter, promenade,
parade of possibilities at play: Sunday
afternoons before tea dance, off-white
evenings kneeling at public urinals, consumed
by what confuses, consuming it
too). Time in its burn is any
life, those hours, afternoons, buildings

smudged with soot and city residues. Later
they take your blood, that tells secrets
it doesn't know, bodies can refuse
their being such, rushing into someone's
wish not to be. My babbling blood.
What's left of burning
burns as well: me down to blackened
glass, an offering in anthracite,
the darkest glitter smoldering underground
until it consumes the earth
which loves me anyway, I'm sure.

The Difficult Music

I started to write a song about you, then I decided, No.
I've been trying to write about violence
for so long. (You were my mother; I love you more
dead. Not a day goes by when I'm not turning someone
into you.) A week of traffic jams and fog
filtered through glass, the country crumbling
in my sleep; old men in plaid jackets on the corner
drinking quart bottles of Old Milwaukee; the color black
again and again.
                  My first summer in Boston
a bum glanced up from tapping at the pavement with a hammer
to whisper Nigger, laughing, when I walked by.
I'd passed the age of consent, I suppose;

my body was never clean again. In Buffalo a billboard
said, "In a dream you saw a way to survive and you woke up
happy," justice talking to the sidewalk on Main Street;
I thought it was talking to me, but it was just
art. (I've wronged too many mornings hallucinating
your voice, too drunk with sleep to understand
the words.)
                    Some afternoons
I can see through a history of heart attacks in two-room
tenement apartments, writing your silted name
on snow with which the lake effect shrouds
a half-abandoned rust belt city. (I've compared you
to snow's unlikely predicates, the moon's
faceless occupation. Some drift
always takes your place.) I was just
scribbling again. Take it from me, my stereo claims, some day
we'll all be free. If anyone should ever write that song.
The finely sifted light falls down.

God-With-Us

after Jean Valentine

What will I call you
when you are gone?
How will I know your name?
Little star, reflection

on the Sea of Galilee,
a lantern in the wood, half-hid,
half-seen?
reflecting on what can't be
touched, be known?
And the sheen of milk
across the sky, the galaxy poured out
like me, true sky, false dawn,
and a young woman's nipple,
star of milk, star of a
nursing child's mouth, my
child, my lord, whoever
you may be today, tonight
which will not end, a cup
passed to me, from which I may
or may not drink, half-empty
star, still asleep by now?
And your small body, Emmanuel,
how small my heart
to fit inside yours)
lie there, pearled, asleep . . .
How I want to believe.
(a pearl, an irritant).

World

for Lawrence White

The man in my dream said, Let me live, but that
was too much of a sacrifice, and I was never
just, like you; he was working for the infidel,
his domino mask said that, blue turban with one
black feather and a ruby set exactly
in the center: entitled to his own sedan chair
with four bearers. An unlikely forebear.
Venice perhaps, betraying anybody's lovers
to sell more of the sea, body of cold
salt water warming in the sun. An heirloom
brooch my mother never owned
is waiting for me when I wake up: Honi soit
qui mal y pense, it says in French that no one
speaks any more, medieval as the patience
it takes to go blind coaxing these raised letters
out of hammered gold and ivory filigree, a full year
of travel and expense: someone waited the entire
fourteenth century for this, no doubt; he's dead
by now, still waiting for that final shipment
from Bukhara, Samarkand, or the Tarim
basin. Shame, indeed. I should think evil of the man
who could command such labor, but
my ancestors weren't involved, and it was
just a gift, passed down like a secret
or a kiss from mouth to mouth: by the time
it's come to me it's been forgotten what it
was, what that man's lips could possibly

have tasted of. Who knows who he stole it
from, who knows who he is now, or
where. This amulet, charm, or medallion
against shames not to be named never was
my mother's, never belonged to anyone
I could mistake for mine. My mother
had nothing she could hand down; I lost it
centuries ago. In my dream he kissed me (I forgot
to say), begged that I not think evil of him
for what he had to take. I won't forgive you, world
I won't survive.

You, Therefore

for Robert Philen

You are like me, you will die too, but not today:
you, incommensurate, therefore the hours shine:
if I say to you "To you I say," you have not been
set to music, or broadcast live on the ghost
radio, may never be an oil painting or
Old Master's charcoal sketch: you are
a concordance of person, number, voice,
and place, strawberries spread through your name
as if it were budding shrubs, how you remind me
of some spring, the waters as cool and clear
(late rain clings to your leaves, shaken by light wind),
which is where you occur in grassy moonlight:
and you are a lily, an aster, white trillium
or viburnum, by all rights mine, white star
in the meadow sky, the snow still arriving
from its earthwards journeys, here where there is
no snow (I dreamed the snow was you,
when there was snow), you are my right,
have come to be my night (your body takes on
the dimensions of sleep, the shape of sleep
becomes you): and you fall from the sky
with several flowers, words spill from your mouth
in waves, your lips taste like the sea, salt-sweet (trees
and seas have flown away, I call it
loving you): home is nowhere, therefore you,
a kind of dwell and welcome, song after all,
and free of any eden we can name.

Karl Tierney

Funereal

In memory of Don Sherrow

One whole ship set with an entire fire,
wasted on a dead Viking.
And now what do we get? Satin in a coffin
and a tombstone that reads "Our Beloved Son"
in English, French, and German
as if you came from a tribe of translators
with aspirations toward the diplomatic corps.
Who knows which is more apropos for laying grave side
flowers of plastic or flowers of silk
when there's not only a new decade and another century
but a fresh millennium just around the corner.

there must've been a cure for the malady or lack of care
or there must be a therapy for the lack of a cure
when I don't know what to wear, beyond black, and
nothing's predictable about fashion except the lack of surprise
particularly when one leaves in a coma
without getting to brush one's teeth.
If we must have ritual,
a pyre of studio junk from the village artist
along with your university diplomas would do.
You've only yourself to blame
that you were no chief, no high priest, no war hero,

and thus we haven't supplied a ship for you
despite your suave, urbane hand in the till of civilization
and your hair cropped as if to say
I'm game, I'm game for anything.

Gertrude Stein to Alice B. Toklas

We are fast
We are fast driving.
Lands unknown.
We fast driving for lands unknown to us.
Our car.
Our car is a Packard.
Our car is a beautiful blue Packard convertible
          and we are fast driving.
Our car is ours, not the bank's,
          and is beautiful and blue
          and we are beautiful and not blue
          and we are fast driving
          and we do not feel a bit dangerous or dirty.
We have the radio on
          and then do not.
First we have the radio on, for the music
          and then we have it off, for the silence.
No! Silence is a lie
          for there is always wind.
We have the sound of wind
          so silence is a lie

when we have the radio off.
In the wind is your red scarf
     and our car is a Packard.
A Packard. Yes, a Packard
     and your red scarf is moving in the wind
     in our beautiful blue Packard convertible.
Your red scarf is moving
     for we are fast driving
     towards lands that do not
     give us a clue of what they might hold.
Fast, yes, fast driving we are
     in a beautiful blue Packard,
     but are neither blue nor worried
     nor very dangerous nor dirty, really.
We are merely fast
     and can be heard with the radio off
     in the sound of the wind.

Jackie O

Every century you get a new facelift
just like Venice, Europe.
Then there you go again
isolating and rude,
denying us even a photograph.

We want to see your cesarean scars.
We want to make a Smithsonian exhibit out of you
climbing on the trunk of a Lincoln convertible.
We want your luncheon remains
with that saliva on it he kissed
or his dry-cleaned brains on that pink suit.
We don't ask what we could do for you
but what you can do for us.
Grant an interview to *Interview*.
Tell us we're selfish.
Tell us we stink.
Tell us we're not like you.

Turning 30

By 30, one discovers there's no age
when one doesn't feel awkward,
just as one finds Great Causes
cannot be swallowed whole,
and no one kisses so divinely
the second time.

What a sign of maturity
to be indifferent to bullying at bus stops or
the bad breath of ogres who like our wounds!
Or jog through Nature with the radio on,
certain that something is familiar but unable
to put its lousy foot forward and shake hands.

We convince ourselves
that Success is a fair trade for Youth.
Pretty Narcissus, petty and vain.
Now there's crow's feet and wisdom
over choosing asparagus spears at the Super
and the Plymouth finally sold
to someone just past half our age
eager to part with what little he has.

George Whitmore

At Seventeen

He is the someone sitting in the background,
in the half-light, insignificant
to the gathering.

                           But his is the smile I
will remember, the smile on the archaic statues
that have survived with no feet or hands.
The statue is in the smile.

It is a face like mine:
never as sensual as now, at seventeen:

                     a point in time marked only
by rapid acceleration, former selves burning off
and bleeding out behind like fire on wings.

There is an acknowledgement
between us that this will always be with us,
                   not like other boys.

                   We do nothing for it,
terrified that it will blossom and blind us.

Aubade

Under the night ceiling the room is still
                      as ocean shelves
with their clutter of frights,
                           outside as far
as stars to drowned men.

I am your willing bed and boat
                         rocking you through
the down driving spiral of sex
                         that wrecked us here.

Awake, not restless, nor in pain
                    I lie senseless
while your breath crawls over me,
                      insensate to
your flesh anchored in me.

Gradually I have learned what the blind know:
                    to ignore the light
near dawn. I concentrate
                    instead on the two

hot compass points of your chest scoring me
                    with the signature
of your discursive dreams.
                    Your heart's faint flywheel
beats against my back;

its perfect mute eloquence steers me
               far out beyond sleep.
The same pump spins the gears
               in you and me and spews

the inks into our every cavity,
               through the vessels
knotted on our bones,
               propels the two-trunked craft
into the sun's snares.

For the sun has a cunning for lovers
               in their conjunctions
and drops down its hooks
               to bring us up dissected.

The slack white ghost of our lovemaking
               churns on to the end
of its tether, the foam
               dancing up in its throat.

The Trucks

The trucks hold a cargo of men
      like the Jews
        who went quietly
(even smiling, nervous).

The trucks are at rest,
      springs swaying
        gently, astonished
headlights open to the empty street.

Somewhere out, way out
      on the highway,
           bearing down on us
                over pylons fisting through the river,
a man drives, holding
      the power of chariots
        in his gloved hands;
it vibrates across his legs.

The trucks rest easy, mindless that I
      am searching
        for that Abednego to fly
through the flames of the furnace with me.

Donald Woods

Sister Lesbos

for Audre

With the smell of last night's love on our lips
our paths collide
Sister Lesbos seeking new love.
Gold studs in the square of your ears
boots like mine

My directions are full of smiles and approval
Sister and brother, brother and sis
smellin love for ourselves
on mornin' lips

I call you sister distinctly, loudly
We are family of a real kind
fruits of the flower pushed sun-ward
through wide cracks in concrete.
March on sister, giving brothers poems
and your sisters that warm love.

What we've shared
is the strength
to be apart
what we seek

is the strength
to be together.
Liberation to love ourselves
fiercely, in the family way.

Subway Trilogy

I.

Ignore the stench of urine
as it travels toward you.
Apologize to the homeless
offering their hunger in outstretched hands.
Watch the closing doors.

Anticipate violence—
To be set upon your brother,
drawing blood for a Walkman,
Tears on the timepiece crystal.
Watch the closing doors.

Whistle away the disdain for your very existence
in the bread winning hours.
For the nocturne sojourn
belongs to you but
Watch the closing doors.

Crowd on, label to label.
Design the disrespect, finger your weapons.
Don't dream, Don't wonder,
Don't think, Don't hope,
Watch the closing doors.

II.

A rage to live, on public transport
I cruise; peruse.
His nature rises to another tune:
Her legs are bare summertime legs,
limbs indeed—dark mahogany
growing from blue denim.
Her breasts point
through cotton, then nylon.

His desire is apparent.
He can flaunt it; he parades it.
With eyelids low, shaded in
cool blue fluorescents, I spy
his flat stomach and smooth extremities.

She rises.
He whispers "negra"
She leaves—wise woman ignores him
while my heart is aflutter,
'cause now we're alone.
He walks toward me.
Sweat collects at my duck lip.

III.

We are villains of the subways
with our dark clothes and eyes,
bloodshot, averted from
beautiful blue-eyed babies
smiling curiously at our massiveness.

We adjust our jewelry,
mined in subjection.
We correct the rakish angle of our hats,
produced in sweatshops in Chinatown.

We read novels that
award chastity with love and
hard work with power.
We sleep to our destination.

BIOGRAPHICAL NOTES

STEVE ABBOTT (1943–1992) was a Renaissance man—poet, novelist, editor, and artist—in the 1970s and 1980s San Francisco literary scene. He edited the magazines *Soup* and *Poetry Flash*, and wrote and illustrated several books of poetry, including *Wrecked Hearts* (Dancing Rock Press, 1978), *Transmuting Gold* (Dancing Rock Press, 1978), *Stretching the Agapé Bra* (Androgyne Press, 1980), and *Skinny Trip to a Far Place* (A. Maciel, 1988) and the bio-poetic fragments in *Lives of the Poets* (Black Star, 1987). He also published two novels, *Holy Terror* (The Crossing Press, 1989) and the posthumous *The Lizard Club* (Autonomedia, 1993), along with the critical essays in *View Askew: Postmodern Investigations* (Androgyne Press, 1989). His daughter, Alysia Abbott, maintains a website in his memory: http://www.steveabbott.org.

REINALDO ARENAS (1943–1990) was persecuted and imprisoned for his writings by Fidel Castro's government. Fleeing Cuba for the United States in 1980 as part of the Mariel Boatlift, he survived to publish such acclaimed novels as *Farewell to the Sea* (Viking, 1986), *Graveyard of the Angels* (Avon, 1987), *Singing from the Well* (Viking, 1987) and *The Palace of the White Skunks* (Viking, 1990). His bestselling autobiography, *Before Night Falls* (Viking, 1993), was adapted into an Academy Award–nominated film in 2000, starring Javier Bardem and Johnny Depp. Collections of his poetry have been published in Spanish as *Voluntad de vivir manifestándose* (Betania, 1989) and *Inferno: poesía completa* (Lumen, 2001).

DAVID CRAIG AUSTIN (1961–1991) published poems in *The Yale Review* and *Poetry East*, among other journals. His work also appeared in *Poets for Life: Seventy-Six Poets Respond to AIDS* (1989). A segment of his poetry library was donated to Poets House in New York City at the time of his death, and in his honor Columbia University bestows the annual David Craig Austin Prize for "the most distinguished thesis in poetry." He completed one manuscript, *The Merciful Country*, which remains unpublished.

THOMAS AVENA (1959–2005) was the founder and editor of *Bastard Review*, a San Francisco literary magazine. Avena's work as an AIDS activist led to profiles in the United States on CNN and ABC News. Additionally, he edited the landmark anthology *Life Sentences: Writers, Artists, and AIDS* (Mercury House, 1994), and with Adam Klein, he co-authored *Jerome: After the Pageant* (Bastard Books, 1996) about the artist and performer Jerome Caja. A poem from his collection *Dream of Order* (Mercury House, 1997) was selected by Adrienne Rich for inclusion in *The Best American Poetry 1996*. A manuscript for a second poetry collection, *Magi*, is still unpublished.

CHARLES BARBER (1956–1992) worked in the theatre and at The Strand bookstore in New York City as a young man. He was later a member of the AIDS poetry workshop that resulted in the anthology *Unending Dialogue* (1991). Selections from correspondence with his friend May Sarton is included in *May Sarton: Selected Letters 1955–1995* (Norton, 2002), and Sarton's letters to Barber are held in the Berg Collection at the New York Public Library. In the words of Sarton, "[Barber] was a poet . . . his death is hard, except that somehow he shines through the darkness."

WILLIAM BARBER (1946–1992) was part of the San Francisco literary scene and published comic erotic novels, including *A Sailor Coming Out* (1972) and *The Chauffeur Did It* (1972), under the pen name "Billy Farout" in the early 1970s. The founder of Farout Press, Barber's poetry collections were *Abyss* (Farout Press/Manroot, 1974) and *Getting Over It: Eight Sonnets* (Hoddypoll Press, 1975). His last published book was the novel *Diary of a New York Queen* (Banned Books, 1988), later produced by actor Harold Finley as a solo stage play; it was performed in London, Edinburgh, and Manchester during the 1993–1994 season.

WALTA BORAWSKI (1947–1994) was a widely published poet active in the Boston poetry scene of the late 1970s and early 1980s, working with the group The Good Gay Poets as well as the Fag Rag collective. His two books are *Sexually Dangerous Poet* (Good Gay Poets, 1984) and *Lingering in a Silk Shirt* (Fag Rag, 1994). Unpublished collections include "St. Theresa of Hemenway Street" and "Opals and Fatimas." Selections from his work also appeared in such anthologies as *A True Likeness: Lesbian & Gay Writing Today* (Sea Horse, 1980), *The Son of the Male Muse* (The Crossing Press, 1983), and *Gay and Lesbian Poetry in Our Time* (St. Martin's, 1988).

WILLIAM BORY (1950–1993) was described by Edmund White as "the American Cavafy," and Edward Lucie-Smith declared his only collection, *Orpheus in His Underwear* (Cythoera, 1993), "one of the most remarkable first books of poetry . . . always exhilarating." The book was nominated for the 1993 Lambda Literary Award in Gay Men's Poetry.

JOE BRAINARD (1942–1994) was a highly acclaimed visual artist and the subject of the 2001–02 celebration "Joe Brainard: A Retrospective," which included exhibitions at the Museum of Modern Art's P.S. 1 Contemporary Art Center. The most recent book of his artwork is *The Nancy Book* (Siglio Press, 2008). His popular memoir in verse, *I Remember* (Angel Hair Books, 1970), was followed by the sequels *More I Remember* (Angel Hair Books, 1972) and *More I Remember More* (Angel Hair Books, 1973), along with *I Remember Christmas* (Museum of Modern Art, 1973). Other books of his writing include *Selected Writing 1962–1971* (Kulchur, 1971) and *Nothing to Write Home About* (Little Caesar Press, 1981). He was the subject of *Joe: A Memoir of Joe Brainard* (Coffee House Press, 2004) by Ron Padgett, who maintains a website devoted to Brainard's life and work: http://www.joebrainard.org.

DONALD BRITTON (1951–1994) published one collection of poetry, *Italy* (Little Caesar, 1981); his second collection, *In the Empire of the Air*, remains unpublished. His essay "The Dark Side of Disneyland" appeared in *Mythomania: Fantasies, Fables, and Sheer Lies in Contemporary American Popular Art* (Art issues. Press, 1996) by Bernard Welt. Reginald Shepherd wrote about Britton in *Contemporary Gay American Poets and Playwrights* (Greenwood, 2003) and was, at the time of his own death, editing *A Kind of Endlessness: Selected Poems of Donald Britton*.

GIL CUADROS (1962–1996) was an active member of the gay community in Los Angeles. Given two years to live by his doctors in 1987, he survived to see the publication of his collection of poetry and stories, *City of God* (City Lights, 1994). The book was called "awesome and haunting" by David Trinidad. He received the 1991 Brody Literature Fellowship. The Gil Cuadros Collection (1990–1993) is housed at UCLA's Chicano Studies Research Center.

SAM D'ALLESANDRO (1956–1988) was the author of a poetry collection, *Slippery Sins* (Ice Press, 1984), and the posthumously published short stories of *The Zombie Pit* (The Crossing Press, 1989), edited by Steve Abbott. Abbott believed that D'Allesandro was "becoming one of the most brilliant writers of his generation" when he died at age 31. Dodie Bellamy collected letters with D'Allesandro into the book *Real: The Letters of Mina Harker and Sam D'Allesandro* (Talisman House, 1994). A book of his collected short stories, *The Wild Creatures* (Suspect Thoughts Press, 2005), was edited by Kevin Killian.

TORY DENT (1958–2005) published three books of poetry before her death: *What Silence Equals* (Persea, 1993), *HIV, Mon Amour* (Sheep Meadow Press, 1999), and *Black Milk* (Sheep Meadow Press, 2005). *HIV, Mon Amour* was nominated for the National Book Critics Circle Award and won the Academy of American Poets' James Laughlin Award. In awarding her the 1999 Laughlin Award, Yusef Komunyakaa called Dent's poetry "a whirlpool of energy . . . painful and truthful, beautiful and terrifying." Her writing about AIDS also appeared in such anthologies as *Life Sentences: Writers, Artists and AIDS* (Mercury House, 1994) and *In the Company of My Solitude* (Persea, 1995). A Guggenheim fellow, Dent was also a widely published art critic.

DANIEL DIAMOND (1949–1996) lived in New York City and was anthologized in *A True Likeness* (Sea Horse Press, 1980), which included his poetic sequence about Isadora Duncan, "True Gesture," and in *The Son of the Male Muse* (The Crossing Press, 1983), containing the seventeen-poem sequence "Dec. 4–8," about a visit home to Michigan. He published numerous limited-edition artist's chapbooks of his poetry, many represented in *Selected Poems (1977–1993)* (1998), edited by Jerry Rosco. Ian Young edited and published Diamond's *Delicious: A Memoir of Glenway Wescott* (Sykes Press) in 2008.

WILLIAM DICKEY (1928–1994) was one of the most award-winning poets of his generation. His first book, *Of the Festivity* (Yale University Press, 1959), was selected by W. H. Auden for the Yale Younger Poets Series. *The Rainbow Grocery* (University of Massachusetts) won the prestigious Juniper Prize in 1978. Widely anthologized and published in literary journals throughout his life, he was for many years professor of English and creative writing at San Francisco State College. Dickey's selected poems, *In the Dreaming* (University of Arkansas), were published in the year of his death. His last book, *The Education of Desire* (Wesleyan) appeared posthumously in 1996.

MELVIN DIXON (1950–1992) was acclaimed both as a poet (*Change of Territory*, 1983) and a novelist (*Trouble the Water*, 1989; *Vanishing Rooms*, 1991). A second, posthumously published collection of poetry, *Love's Instruments* (Tia Chucha), was released in 1995. As a translator, Dixon published *The Collected Poems of Léopold Sédhar Senghor* (University Press of Virginia, 1991), and he served as a professor at Williams College and Queens College of the City University of New York. In 2006, the University Press of Mississippi published a collection of his essays, *A Melvin Dixon Critical Reader*, edited by Dwight McBride and Justin Joyce.

TIM DLUGOS (1950–1990) was a prominent younger poet who was active in both the Mass Transit poetry scene in Washington, D.C. in the early 1970s and New York's downtown literary scene in the late seventies and eighties. His books include *Je Suis Ein Americano* (Little Caesar Press, 1979), *A Fast Life* (Sherwood Press, 1982), and *Entre Nous* (Little Caesar, 1982). In 1996, David Trinidad edited *Powerless*, Dlugos's selected poems, for High Risk Books. A comprehensive edition of Dlugos's poems, *A Fast Life: Poems of Tim Dlugos*, edited by Trinidad, is forthcoming from Nightboat Books in 2011.

JIM EVERHARD (1946–1986) was a Washington D.C. area resident, where he attended George Mason University. He published one book of poems, *Cute* (Gay Sunshine Press, 1982), which was lauded by poet and editor Ron Schreiber as "a marvelous book . . . rich and funny, deeply moving." His work was also featured in the anthology *Gay Roots, Vol. 2* (Gay Sunshine Press, 1993). At his death, he was working on an unfinished novel, "Three Weeks at the Heart of an Empire." Winston Leyland, founder and publisher of Gay Sunshine Press (www.gaysunshinepress.com), is currently preparing an in-depth book of his poems, published and unpublished.

DON GARNER (1945–1989) sold his poetry in the form of chapbooks and broadsides on the streets of Toronto in the early 1980s. Garner would finance living and writing in the winter in Toronto by working as a geophysicist in the Yukon during the summer months. Garner's Huron Path Press published the literary magazine *Up Front*, as well as his four chapbooks: *Dirty Laundry* (1978), *Yukon Violation* (1979), *Running Sore* (1980), and *Pretend You're Still Alive* (1981). His work also appeared in *The Body Politic*.

CHASEN GAVER (1953–1989), a Washington D.C.-based performance poet, published work in many magazines, including *The James White Review* and *Mouth of the Dragon*. He appeared on film in *Beat: The Performance Poetry of Chasen Gaver* (1984) and on the audiocassette releases *Daddy!* and *Personality Cult*. His comic mystery novel/picture book, *The Party's Over* (Consciousness Squared Communications, 1985), chronicled the D.C. party scene of the late 1970s. Gaver was the first openly gay recipient of a grant from the D.C. Commission for the Arts and Humanities. Many of his papers and writings are held in the Cornell University Archives.

RICHARD GEORGE-MURRAY (1927–2008) was an aficionado of the short-form poem. He practiced this art in more than two dozen handmade artist's chapbooks, most issued through Primrose Apathy Press. These include *Markings* (1976, revised 1981), *Lilac Cure* (1981), *This Playground Closes at Dusk* (1982), and *Hop on the Running Board and I'll Give You a Lift* (1983). Ian Young edited George-Murray's *Yes is Such a Long Word: Selected Poems* (Entimos Press, 1995).

JAIME GIL DE BIEDMA (1929–1990) is considered the most significant Spanish poet since the Spanish Civil War. A gay, leftist poet from Barcelona, he wrote cosmopolitan, politically committed poetry and was associated with the '50s Generation of writers who opposed the Franco dictatorship. He worked most of his life at the

Philippine Tobacco Company on Las Ramblas in Barcelona. His life is detailed in Miguel Dalmau's biography *Jaime Gil de Biedma* (Circe, 2004) and his poems are collected in *Las personas del verbo* (Seix Barral, 1982). James Nolan has translated Gil de Biedma's poetry in *Longing: Selected Poems* (City Lights Books, 1993).

ROY GONSALVES (1959–1993) was an African American poet and artist who published his work in *Evening Sunshine* (1988) and *Perversion* (Renaissance Press, 1990), which was nominated for the Gregory Kolovakos Award for AIDS Writing in 1991. His poems appeared in such anthologies as *The Road Before Us* (Galiens Press, 1991) and *Sojourner: Black Gay Voices in the Age of AIDS* (Other Countries, 1993). Gonsalves was also associated with the Other Countries black gay writing collective.

CRAIG G. HARRIS (1958–1991) worked as a reporter for his hometown *New York Native* and as an editor with a variety of publishing houses, including Avon, Bantam, and Scholastic. He was one of five gay African American poets anthologized in *Tongues Untied* (GMP, 1987). His poetry, fiction, and essays appeared in such newspapers and magazines as *Blackheart*, *The Philadelphia Tribune*, *Black/Out*, *Gay Community News*, and *RFD*, and in the anthologies *In the Life* (Alyson, 1986), *Brother to Brother* (Alyson, 1991), and *The Road Before Us* (Galiens, 1991). His work appeared posthumously in *Sojourner: Black Gay Voices in the Age of AIDS* (Other Countries, 1993).

ESSEX HEMPHILL (1957–1995), a Washington D.C. native, achieved renown for both his poetry and essays. In addition to self-created artist's books like *Plums* and *Diamonds Was in the Kitty*, Hemphill published chapbooks—*Earth Life* (Be Bop Books,

1985) and *Conditions* (Be Bop Books, 1986)—and his poems and essays were collected in *Ceremonies* (Plume, 1992). He edited the black gay anthology *Brother to Brother: New Writings by Black Gay Men* (Alyson) in 1991. Hemphill appeared in Marlon Riggs's controversial, award-winning films *Black Is/Black Ain't* (1994) and *Tongues Untied* (1990) and his poetry was included in Isaac Julien's *Looking for Langston* (1989).

LELAND HICKMAN (1934–1991) was a Los Angeles-area modernist poet who helped the Language Poetry movement achieve a wider audience. He published the books *Tiresias I:9:B: Great Slave Lake Suite* (Momentum Press, 1980)—which was a finalist for the 1980 *Los Angeles Times* Book Prize—and *Lee Sr Falls to the Floor* (Jahbone, 1991). Hickman served as editor and printer for the poetry magazine *Temblor*, editor of the literary journal *Bachy*, and co-founder of Littoral Press. Many of his papers can be found at the University of California, San Diego. Nightboat Books published *Tiresias: The Collected Poems of Leland Hickman* in 2009.

JAMES S HOLMES (1924–1986) published his poetry in *Early Verse, 1947–1957* (C. J. Aarts, 1985). As Jim Holmes, he also released poems in *9 Hidebound Rimes* (Pink Triangle Poets, 1978) and as "Jacob Lowland" in *The Gay Stud's Guide to Amsterdam and Other Sonnets* (C. J. Aarts, 1978). A U.S. native and a respected translator and teacher at the University of Amsterdam, Holmes helped establish the discipline of Gay Studies in the Netherlands. He co-edited *Dutch Interiors: Postwar Poetry of the Netherlands and Flanders* (Columbia University Press, 1984) and a posthumous collection of his essays, *Translated: Papers on Literary Translation and Translation Studies* (Editions Rodophi) appeared in 1988.

ARTURO ISLAS (1938–1991) was the author of novels exploring the Mexican-American experience, including a trilogy comprising *The Rain God* (Alexandrian Press, 1984), *Migrant Souls* (William Morrow, 1990) and the posthumously published *La Mollie and the King of Tears* (University of New Mexico, 1996). *Migrant Souls* was the first novel by a Chicano author to be published by a major New York publishing house. Islas was a student and later professor at Stanford University, which currently holds his papers in its library of special collections. Scholar Frederick Luis Aldama edited *Arturo Islas: The Uncollected Works* (Arte Público Press, 2003) and wrote a biography of Islas, *Dancing with Ghosts* (University of California, 2004).

ADAM JOHNSON (1965–1993) died when he was only 28, but before his death, he wrote and published multiple chapbooks and full-length collections, beginning with the self-published *In the Garden* (1986) and continuing through *Poems* (Hearing Eye, 1992), *The Spiral Staircase* (Acumen, 1993), and *The Playground Bell* (Carcanet, 1994). Neil Powell edited his *Collected Poems* (Carcanet, 2003) and called Johnson "one of those rare beings who, through their work and their presence, truly sustain a culture."

GLENN PHILIP KRAMER (1953?–1991?) was a member of the AIDS poetry workshop that resulted in the anthology *Unending Dialogue* (1991).

MICHAEL LYNCH (1944–1991) was an academic, teaching modern poetry and fiction at the University of Toronto, and the author of *These Waves of Dying Friends* (Contact II Publications, 1989). For many years, he was a regular contributor to *The Body Politic*, and the founder of a number of key HIV/AIDS organizations in

Toronto, including the AIDS Committee of Toronto, the AIDS Memorial, and AIDS Action Now. His writings on AIDS, according to Gerald Hannon, "contributed to the more humane, less panic-stricken response to the disease in Canada." He was the subject of Ann Silversides's book *AIDS Activist: Michael Lynch and the Politics of Community* (Between the Lines, 2003).

PAUL MARIAH (1937–1996) was widely published in periodicals, including every significant gay literary magazine, among them *Gay Sunshine, Mouth of the Dragon, One,* and *Sebastian Quill.* He was also a contributor to the anthologies *The Male Muse* (The Crossing Press, 1973) and *Angels of the Lyre* (Gay Sunshine Press, 1975). His books and chapbooks include *Personae Non Gratae* (Shameless Hussy Press, 1971), poems about his time in prison for "homosexual offences"; *Letter to Robert Duncan While Bending the Bow* (ManRoot, 1974); and *This Light Will Spread: Selected Poems 1960–1975* (ManRoot, 1978). He founded *ManRoot* magazine and directed ManRoot Press from 1969 until his death. Those interested in more information about Mariah's books may contact his sister and executor, Mary Alice Sims, at 618–438–9700.

DAVID MATIAS (1961–1996), born David Rodriguez, published poetry during his lifetime in *Dances with Family and Disease* (1993) and posthumously in *Fifth Season* (Provincetown Arts Press, 1998) and the anthology *Things Shaped in Passing* (Persea, 1997). He was also heavily involved in theater in his adopted hometown of Provincetown. Former U.S. Poet Laureate Robert Pinsky called Matias's poems "splendid" and *Fifth Season* "a rich, deeply intelligent book, a triumph of art and feeling."

JAMES MERRILL (1926–1995) was the recipient of many awards for his poetry, included the National Book Award and the Pulitzer Prize. He published over twenty books, and has been the subject of multiple works of criticism, including Stephen Yenser's *The Consuming Myth: The Work of James Merrill* (Harvard University Press, 1987). His best known books include *Nights and Days* (Atheneum, 1966), *Braving the Elements* (Atheneum, 1972), *Divine Comedies* (Atheneum, 1976), and his epic *The Changing Light at Sandover* (Atheneum, 1982). J. D. McClatchy and Stephen Yenser edited Merrill's *Collected Poems* (Knopf, 2001), *Collected Novels and Plays* (Knopf, 2002), and *Collected Prose* (Knopf, 2004). Merrill was both a member of the Academy of American Arts and Letters and a chancellor of the Academy of American Poets.

PAUL MONETTE (1945–1995) was the first openly gay writer to win the National Book Award, for his memoir *Becoming a Man* (Harcourt Brace Jovanovich, 1992). His other award-winning works of nonfiction include *Borrowed Time* (Harcourt Brace Jovanovich, 1988) and *Last Watch of the Night* (Harcourt Brace Jovanovich, 1994), one essay from which, "The Politics of Silence," Monette delivered as part of the Library of Congress's National Book Week Lecture Series. He also published six novels and four books of poetry, including *No Witnesses* (Avon, 1981) his acclaimed *Love Alone: 18 Elegies for Rog* (St. Martin's, 1988), and *West of Yesterday, East of Summer: New and Selected Poems (1973–1993)* (St. Martin's, 1994).

COOKIE MUELLER (1949–1989), a Baltimore native, first came to attention acting in John Waters's films, including *Multiple*

Maniacs (1970), *Pink Flamingos* (1972), *Female Trouble* (1974), and *Desperate Living* (1977). She wrote art criticism for *Details* and a health advice column, "Ask Dr. Mueller," for the *East Village Eye*. Her books included *How to Get Rid of Pimples* (Top Stories, 1984); *Fan Mail, Frank Letters, and Crank Calls* (Hanuman, 1988); *Garden of Ashes* (Hanuman, 1990); and *Walking Through Clear Water in a Pool Painted Black* (Semiotext(e), 1990). Much of this material was gathered in *Ask Dr. Mueller: The Writings of Cookie Mueller* (High Risk Books/Serpent's Tail, 1997), edited by Amy Scholder.

J. M. REGAN (1947–1991?), educated at City University of New York and Georgetown University, was both a writing instructor at City University of New York and a chef. Many of Regan's poems were published in *The James White Review*. He was also anthologized in *Gay and Lesbian Poetry in Our Time* (1988) and *Poets for Life: Seventy-Six Poets Respond to AIDS* (1989).

RICHARD RONAN (1946-1989) published six books of poetry, including *Narratives from America* (Dragon Gate, 1982). Many of his books, such as *A Radiance Like Wind or Water* (Dragon Gate, 1984) and *Buddha's Kisses* (Gay Sunshine Press, 1980), were influenced by his longtime interest in Eastern culture and religion. His poetic cycle *Flowers* (Calamus, 1978), featuring illustrations from longtime collaborator Bill Rancitelli, was performed at The Glines in New York City, among other venues. Ronan was also involved in writing for the avant-garde theater and founded and directed a school for special needs high school students. He is the subject of the short biography *Richard Ronan* by Jan VanStavern (Boise State University, 1996).

Assotto Saint (1957–1994) was an influential poet, editor, and publisher born in Haiti. He published two collections of poems: *Stations* (Galiens, 1989) and *Wishing for Wings* (Galiens, 1994). As founder of Galiens Press, he promoted black gay poetry by editing the anthologies *The Road Before Us* (1991), which won the Lambda Literary Award for gay men's poetry and was nominated for the 1992 ALA Stonewall Book Award, and *Here to Dare* (1992). Saint was also a successful playwright (*Risin' to the Love We Need*) and songwriter (with his band Xotica). After his death, all of his known published and unpublished work was gathered in *Spells of a Voodoo Doll* (Richard Kasak Books/Masquerade, 1996).

Paul Schmidt (1934–1999) wrote the books *Night Life* and *Winter Solstice* (both from Painted Leaf Press, 1996) and the introduction to photographer Robert Mapplethorpe's notorious *X Portfolio* (1978). He was the translator of *The Complete Works of Arthur Rimbaud* (Harper & Row, 1976), *The Collected Works of Velimir Khlebnikov* (Harvard University Press, 1989), and *The Plays of Anton Chekhov* (HarperCollins, 1997). An additional volume of Schmidt's Rimbaud translations, *A Season in Hell*, featuring Mapplethorpe's photographs, appeared in a limited edition in 1986 and a trade edition in 1997. Married for seven years to actress Stockard Channing, Schmidt appeared in such films as *Swoon* (1992) and *Six Degrees of Separation* (1993).

Jack Sharpless (1950–1988) published no poetry during his lifetime, but his sequence *Inroads*, dramatic monologues by the dying Queen Elizabeth I, was awarded England's prestigious Duncan Lawrie Prize in 1985. Other sequences include *Quantum: The Lost Sybilline Books* (1977–78) and *The Fall of the X Dynasty*

(1981–84). Ronald Johnson edited *Presences of Mind: The Collected Books of Jack Sharpless* (Gnomon, 1989), which was published posthumously and featured discussions of Sharpless's work by Johnson, Guy Davenport, and Jonathan Williams.

REGINALD SHEPHERD (1963–2008) was a professor at Cornell University and a widely published poet. His collections of poetry were *Some Are Drowning* (1994); *Angel, Interrupted* (1996); *Wrong* (1999); *Otherhood* (2003); and *Fata Morgana* (2007), all from University of Pittsburgh Press. As an editor, he compiled the books *The Iowa Anthology of New American Poetries* (University of Iowa, 2004) and *Lyric Postmodernisms* (Counterpath, 2008), and his essay collection *Orpheus in the Bronx: Essays on Identity, Politics, and the Freedom of Poetry* (University of Michigan Press, 2008) was nominated for a National Book Critics Circle Award for criticism. Another book of poems will be published posthumously.

KARL TIERNEY (1956–1995) was born in Westfield, Massachusetts, and raised in Connecticut and Louisiana. An Emory graduate, he completed an MFA in creative writing at the University of Arkansas in 1982 and within a year moved to San Francisco. A chapbook, *Billy Idol's Birthday* (Arroyo-Sheldon), appeared in 1993. Though he had yet to publish a full-length book, more than fifty of his poems appeared in magazines and anthologies during his lifetime. He was twice a finalist for the Walt Whitman Award, a finalist for the National Poetry Series, and a Yaddo fellow. Sick and seriously depressed, he took his own life in October of 1995. A book-length selection, titled *Castro Poems*, awaits a publisher. Those interested in seeing the manuscript should contact his literary executor, Jim Cory, at coryjim@earthlink.net.

GEORGE WHITMORE (1946–1989) was best known as a novelist and member of the famed Violet Quill gay writing collective. Before gaining a reputation for his fiction and journalism, he published two short collections of poetry, *Tricking* (Free Milk Fund Press, 1974) and *Getting Gay in New York* (Free Milk Fund Press, 1976). His novels were *The Confessions of Danny Slocum* (St. Martin's, 1980) and *Nebraska* (Grove, 1987). He also published one volume of nonfiction, *Someone Was Here: Profiles in the AIDS Epidemic* (New American Library, 1988). Work by Whitmore both published and unpublished was anthologized in *The Violet Quill Reader* (St. Martin's, 1994), edited by David Bergman.

DONALD W. WOODS (1958–1992) was involved in the Other Countries and Blackheart Collective gay writing groups. He published one chapbook/portfolio, *The Space* (1989), and was anthologized in *In the Life* (Alyson, 1986), *Brother to Brother* (Alyson, 1991), *The Road Before Us* (Galiens, 1992), and *Sojourner: Black Gay Voices in the Age of AIDS* (Other Countries, 1993). Woods's work as an AIDS activist in the African American community included developing AIDS prevention films, and he appeared posthumously in Marlon Riggs's documentary *No Regret* (1993).

TRANSLATORS

Dolores M. Koch (1928–2009) (translator for Reinaldo Arenas), born in Cuba, was a widely published scholar of Latin American literature, including influential work on the genre of the *microrrelato*. Her many translations from the Spanish include writing by Jorge Bucay, Alina Fernanez, Laura Restrepo, Emilie Schindler, and Reinaldo Arenas's memoir, *Before Night Falls* (Viking, 1993). Her most recent translation was Enrique Joven's *The Book of God and Physics* (William Morrow, 2009), published just weeks before her death. She received her doctorate in Latin American Literature from the City University of New York in 1986.

Jaime Manrique (translator for Reinaldo Arenas) is a Colombian poet, novelist, essayist, and translator who has written in both English and Spanish and whose work has been translated into many languages. Among his publications are the volumes of poems *My Night with Federico García Lorca* (Groundwater, 1995) and *Tarzan, My Body, Christopher Columbus* (Painted Leaf, 2001); the novels *Colombian Gold* (Clarkson N. Potter, 1983), *Latin Moon in Manhattan* (St. Martin's, 1992), *Twilight at the Equator* (Faber & Faber, 1997), and *Our Lives Are the Rivers* (HarperCollins, 2006); and the memoir *Eminent Maricones: Arenas, Lorca, Puig, and Me* (University of Wisconsin, 1999). His honors include Colombia's National Poetry Award, the 2007 International Latino Book Award for Best Historical Novel, and a Guggenheim Fellowship. From 2002 to 2008, Manrique was associate professor in the MFA program in writing at Columbia University. He is a Trustee of PEN American Center.

JAMES NOLAN (translator for Jaime Gil de Biedma) won the 2007 Jefferson Prize for his most recent book, *Perpetual Care: Stories* (Jefferson Press, 2008). His collections of poetry are *Why I Live in the Forest* (Wesleyan, 1974) and *What Moves Is Not the Wind* (Wesleyan, 1980). He has also translated Pablo Neruda's *Stones of the Sky* (Copper Canyon Press, 1987). He has been honored by two Fulbright fellowships to Spain, where he lived and taught during ten years. He now directs the Loyola Writing Institute in his native New Orleans. His post-Katrina novel *Higher Ground* was awarded the 2008 William Faulkner-Wisdom Prize.

COPYRIGHT STATEMENTS